Praise for *Keep Breathing*

"No one escapes dealing with loss, and when the loss is unthinkable, the journey can be both long and difficult. This is a story about unimaginable grief that lands on a mind already acquainted with trauma. Dr. Kate Truitt, as both a trauma expert and survivor, provides a firsthand, scientific account of what drove her thoughts and behavior in seeking a cure for her suffering. An amazing story, an enlightening read, and a remarkable ending. For those on this healing journey or those who know someone who is, consider this book aspirational."

—**Ronald Ruden, MD, PhD,** creator of the Havening Techniques® and author of *The Craving Brain* and *When the Past Is Always Present: Emotional Traumatization, Causes, and Cures*

"*Keep Breathing* by Dr. Kate Truitt is a whirlwind of emotional honesty and intellectual bravery. This book takes readers on a roller coaster ride through the highs and lows of human experience, combining Dr. Truitt's personal trials with her scientific expertise. Her writing style is unorthodox yet utterly captivating, turning a story of personal grief into a beacon of hope for anyone in the throes of life's chaos. This book doesn't just share a story; it dares readers to confront their own vulnerabilities and emerge stronger, armed with a deeper understanding of the mind and heart."

—**Frank G. Anderson, MD,** internationally renowned trauma expert and author of *To Be Loved* and *Transcending Trauma*

"Dr. Kate Truitt's new book is a deeply moving memoir and a perfect complement to her first book, *Healing in Your Hands*. Within these pages, she shares her personal story of tragic loss and the posttraumatic stress that encompasses her life following that fateful day. For those of us who are trauma survivors, these words help us feel less alone and deeply understood. The story continues as a beacon of hope as you, too, will discover the transformational power of Havening Touch® techniques and how they allow you to tap into the healing potential that lives within us all."

—**Arielle Schwartz, PhD,** author of *The Post-Traumatic Growth Guidebook* and *The Complex PTSD Workbook*

"*Keep Breathing* by Dr. Kate Truitt is a poignant narrative that gracefully intertwines the threads of personal tragedy and scientific exploration. Following her own experience of deep loss, Dr. Truitt examines the facets of trauma, the impacts of childhood, and the struggle with depression, leading readers on a journey toward understanding and resilience. Her story is a testament to the human spirit's ability to not only endure but also find meaning, hope, and growth in the face of adversity. This book stands as a powerful example of how personal loss can illuminate the path to self-discovery and healing."

—**Claire Bidwell Smith, LCPC,** author of *Anxiety: The Missing Stage of Grief* and *Anxious Grief*

"In *Keep Breathing*, Dr. Kate Truitt presents a daring and insightful narrative. This book blends a gripping story of personal loss with laser-sharp technical insights about the brain and nervous system. It's a candid, almost provocative invitation to peer into the abyss of trauma and emerge hopeful."

—**Annie Chen, LMFT,** author of *The Attachment Theory Workbook* and *I Want to Connect*

"'Never underestimate your ability to experience the darkness and still shine on.' This book contains the message needed for this tumultuous time in our existence. Dr. Truitt has given us a unique opportunity to walk alongside her personal tragedy, hand in hand with the neuroscience of what happens in the brain. A must-read that has changed my life for the better."

—**Scarlett Lewis,** founder and chief movement officer at the Jesse Lewis Choose Love Movement, international author, and recipient of the International Forgiveness Award, Peace Hero Award, and Common Ground Award, among others

"A riveting and fascinating book! Dr. Truitt's story is inspiring and courageous and gives tremendous hope to people who are recovering from trauma. Everyone should read this book. Once I started, I literally couldn't put it down."

—**David Granirer,** founder, Stand Up For Mental Health™

"Dr. Truitt's vulnerable exposure of her personal narrative places her wisdom around the neurophysiology of trauma within a concrete framework. Her ability to describe severe stress through its profound chronological impact on her own life and then zoom out to a wider lens of how humans are affected makes the science personal. She models self-compassion, curiosity, and perseverance in a way that only a clinical psychologist and applied neuroscientist with trauma can, learning through her past. Her description of her healing journey and the changes she experiences in her mind-body system is a moving, heart-warming experience. We root for her the way she roots for us all."

—**Christine Gibson, MD,** author of *The Modern Trauma Toolkit: Nurture Your Post-Traumatic Growth with Personalized Solutions*, @TikTokTraumaDoc, and co-founder of the Safer Spaces Training Program

"This is the only book that walks you through the depths of a deeply traumatic event and gives you insight on the neuroscience that is controlling what Kate and others experience. Oftentimes we want to believe we know what is happening to us when we go through trauma. The truth is we don't know the depths of our habits, systems, and repetitive thoughts. This book lays out a path for people to see themselves and the real-life skills they can build to begin to heal the trauma in their lives."

—**Ross Szabo,** wellness director at Geffen Academy at UCLA, CEO of the Human Power Project, and author of *A Kids Book About Anxiety*

"*Keep Breathing* by Dr. Kate Truitt is a moving testament to the resilience of the human spirit, expertly blending her own journey of loss and recovery with her neuroscience background. This book provides a compassionate and empathetic yet scientifically grounded guide for anyone navigating the challenging path of emotional healing. Dr. Truitt's narrative is both touching and informative, serving as a source of comfort and understanding for those facing life's most difficult moments. It's a compelling and moving invitation to find strength and renewal in the midst of adversity. I am so moved by her powerful testimony and her ability to access words to describe life's unthinkable moments and to light a path for so many finding their way through the nonlinear journey of healing. Dr. Truitt is a gift and light in this world and provides a safe haven for all those longing to be seen in their grief."

—**Zahabiyah Yamasaki, MEd, RYT,** author of *Trauma-Informed Yoga for Survivors of Sexual Assault* and *Your Joy Is Beautiful*

"Bold, honest, relatable, informative, and brave are a few words to describe Dr. Kate Truitt's riveting new book, *Keep Breathing*. Truitt beautifully weaves her personal story with easily digestible neuroscience, helping us understand how our brains work and inviting us to learn to partner with our amygdala rather than fighting against it. As a certified trauma therapist, I can't recommend this book enough—not only to the mental health community and their clients but to anyone who has been through something hard in their life and wants to reach the other side. *Keep Breathing* should be on every bookshelf!"

—**Susan Zinn, LPCC, LMHC, NCC,** founder of Westside Counseling Center, best-selling co-author of *The Epiphanies Project*, and the recipient of President Obama's Volunteer Service Award

"Dr. Truitt's masterful book, *Keep Breathing*, reads like *Lessons in Chemistry* for neuroscience and trauma. Heartbreaking, courageous, ultimately hopeful and uplifting, this book of brain healing and redemption is a surprise page-turner. I couldn't put it down."

—**Leslie Glass,** author of *The Mother-Daughter Relationship Makeover*

"In her newest book, *Keep Breathing*, Dr. Kate Truitt masterfully intertwines her own poignant story of loss with her extensive knowledge of the brain's workings. This narrative serves as a powerful ally to those wrestling with the weight of emotional trauma. Dr. Truitt's book is a lighthouse in the storm for readers, offering a unique combination of heartfelt experience and scientific exploration. It is an essential read for anyone seeking to understand the complexities of healing and personal transformation."

—**Courtney Armstrong, PhD,** author of *Rethinking Trauma Treatment*

"*Keep Breathing* is a gorgeous mosaic of life's ups and downs. It is a stand-out book that beautifully weaves Dr. Kate's poignant and vulnerable stories together with the science and psychology behind what is actually going on in our bodies and brains all the while. Her intimate knowledge of the neuroscience of trauma, combined with her personal experience, has given her unique insights to help others overcome their own traumas. Whether you are looking to get relief in your own life or are a practitioner leading or supporting others, *Keep Breathing* will give you valuable tools and stories to help you move forward in your journey."

—**Laura Haver,** author of *Play Together* and founder of Author Moms

"Prepare to be captivated as Dr. Kate Truitt expertly guides you on a remarkable journey, seamlessly inviting the reader to walk alongside her as she rises from the depths of despair to build a purpose-driven, fulfilled life. With skill and grace, she weaves the intricate tapestry of neurobiology into the fabric of real-world trauma-induced emotional distress. Dr. Truitt's unique perspective as both an active participant and a keen observer offers poignant insights into the limitations of our current knowledge. Dr. Truitt's narrative unfolds with a riveting, page-turning style that touches our deepest emotions from hopelessness and loss to the triumphant reclamation of her authentic self. Driven by an unyielding desire not just to survive but to thrive, this story serves as a beacon of hope and understanding for those grappling with the life-altering burden of traumatic stress."

—**Steven J. Ruden, DDS,** co-founder and
developer of the Havening Techniques

"*Keep Breathing* is the poignant true story of Dr. Kate Truitt's 'phoenix journey' through PTSD. Struck by unforeseen grief just before her wedding, Truitt confronts the waves of pain and the 'profound powerlessness' her own brain subjects her to. Her narrative, resonating with Dr. Jill Bolte Taylor's *My Stroke of Insight*, is both a deeply personal tale and a beacon for those touched by trauma. Truitt stands as a guide through the darkness of PTSD, using her expertise to illuminate the path to recovery. This book will change how we perceive pain and human resilience.

—**John Freedom, CEHP,** research coordinator for the
Association for Comprehensive Energy Psychology, member
of the board of trustees for EFT International, and author
of *Heal Yourself with Emotional Freedom Technique*

"Dr. Kate Truitt pens like a fast-paced novel but with an important catch. She has created a captivating autobiographical piece of literature, courageously exposing wounds from several painful PTSD occurrences. Yet, as a neuroscientist, traumatologist, and psychologist, she peppers neuroscientific explanations, research citations, and contemporary metaphorical clarification throughout her narrative. This book has double benefit, as she explores flawed human conditions while maintaining a keen observing clinical eye. I was spellbound by her grueling, gritty story, resonated with her dance to survive, admired her tenacity, then paused to grasp neuroscientific constructs. This book belongs in the heart, mind, and hand of anyone seeking knowledge about, recovering from, or treating PTSD."

—**Robin Bilazarian, LCSW, DCSW, DCEP,** international certified master EFT trainer and author of *Tapping the Mighty Mind: Simple Solutions for Stress, Conflict, and Pain*

"In *Keep Breathing*, Dr. Kate Truitt courageously takes the reader through the dark forest of her own path in search of an answer. One might reasonably consider Kate a modern-day mythological warrior. Severely emotionally wounded in battle with a crushing traumatic experience, she rose to subdue and even conquer the evil spell of trauma threatening the land. Mastering the magic, she brings back to the world the knowledge of trauma's mechanism. Like a true hero, she also brings back the prize, a protocol to help free those lost to trauma and the recognition that 'the Self can be one thing and the brain another.' Gracefully, intelligently, movingly told."

—**Judith Simon Prager, PhD,** co-author of *The Worst Is Over: What to Say When Every Moment Counts* and *Verbal First Aid*

"This remarkably powerful memoir offers a unique lens of compassion toward our brain's efforts to keep us alive and safe. Shared with exquisite vulnerability, Dr. Kate Truitt's deeply personal journey is raw, wrenching, and transformative, illuminated by neuroscience made accessible with endearing warmth. For readers who resonate—due to trauma, grief, loss, or childhood adversities—with the constant search for peace and maybe even purpose, *Keep Breathing* extends from a place of undeniable authenticity perhaps the most rare and elusive of gifts: hope."

—**Joy Thomas,** director of communications and community engagement, ACE Resource Network

KEEP
BREATHING
KEEP
BREATHING
KEEP
BREATHING

**A PSYCHOLOGIST'S INTIMATE JOURNEY THROUGH
LOSS, TRAUMA, AND REDISCOVERING LIFE**

Kate Truitt, PhD

KEEP BREATHING
Copyright © 2024 by Kate Truitt

Published by
Bridge City Books, an imprint of PESI Publishing, Inc.
3839 White Ave
Eau Claire, WI 54703

Cover and interior design by Amy Rubenzer

The cover showcases *Possibilities*, a painting created by author
Kate Truitt in 2009, serving as a symbol of hope during her
darkest moments of despair.

Editing by Chelsea Thompson

ISBN: 9781962305099 (print)
ISBN: 9781962305365 (ePDF)
ISBN: 9781962305105 (ePUB)

Bridge City Books
An Imprint of PESI Publishing

To my village, my Odyssey—may we continue to rise.
Phoenix Up!

Table of Contents

Introduction

Welcome.

This book is my story of moving through the depths of darkness that consumed me in the years after my fiancé suddenly passed away, just one week before our wedding. It's an account of the years of trauma I endured long before my fiancé's death. It's a neuroscientific examination of how the brain uses our past to inform the present. Part autobiography and part scientific exploration, this book uses my story as a case study to illuminate the common experiences in the human brain—deep love and devastating loss, exhilaration and pain, life and death—that have the power to both derail our lives and build our empowered futures.

Over the course of writing this book, I have had many people ask me why I would share my story in such a public way. Ultimately, the answer is simple: I've done it so people know they are not alone. Despite having studied fear and trauma for almost a decade before my journey with PTSD began, I was shocked by the profound powerlessness I experienced. I often felt crazy, scared, and helpless as my brain did things beyond my control. Reducing shame about these very weird, very human moments through openness, sharing stories, and education is a significant motivator for me, both in writing this book and for my life in general.

But this book is more than a survival story. It's a love story, though certainly not the traditional kind. Rather, it is a love story about coming back to Self. It's about leaning into the darkest hours of our lives and inviting the people who love us to walk through the darkness with us. It's about the parts of our brains that can cause immeasurable pain but also create our most vibrant opportunities to thrive. Ultimately, it's about the capacity of humans to endure the "phoenix journey"—flying into the flames only to rise up from the ashes stronger than before.

These pages will bring you along with me through my own phoenix journey—from being gutted and broken to learning how I could adapt to survive what seemed to be permanently encoded traumas. Along the way, you will learn about the neuroscience around trauma and stress. You will learn a lot about the amygdalae, the tiny structures in the brain that play a vital role in helping us survive and thrive. You'll also see how the brain can get so easily confused and misconstrue data in our day-to-day lives, causing massive disruptions—PTSD, rage, suicidal thoughts, depression, gastrointestinal problems, inflammation, panic, high blood pressure, cardiac concerns, and so much more. Most importantly, you'll learn how the amygdalae act without conscious awareness of the present moment, defining our choices before our conscious Self has time to weigh in.

Ultimately, this story is meant to help you tap into the process of the phoenix journey. I want people to know they have the opportunity to heal. My deepest desire for this book is for people to move into understanding, empathy, and compassion for how their past impacts the way they are living and to help others—*you*—learn to be proactive in finding opportunities for empowerment and strength, even in our darkest moments. Our brains carry within them the capacity to heal; sometimes we just don't know it.

Note to the Reader

"First the pain, then the waiting, then the rising."

—Glennon Doyle, *Untamed*

Before we get started, a loving disclaimer:

While this book is a story of love, and ultimately strength, it's a strange one. The initial chapters are genuine and very painful. They were often difficult to write, and at times, they may be difficult to read.

I have worked hard to contextualize my story in the best way I know how: through the lens of science, healing, and the ability to thrive (also known as posttraumatic growth). But science does not—and cannot—change reality. The next few chapters are the "being in" of the trauma and pain. Please take care while reading.

With warmth and healing,

Kate

CHAPTER 1

A Confluence of Events

"Breath is the bridge which connects life to consciousness,
which unites your body to your thoughts."

—Thích Nhất Hạnh

We all have moments in life that create an irreversible chasm between what was and what will be. Mine happened when I was only twenty-nine years old, on a warm day in June, the so-perfect-it's-cliché time for weddings. The chapel is packed beyond standing room with people; they've overflowed into the parking lot. There are flowers all around me. Soft music plays as guests greet each other in a reverent hush.

All of this was meant for my wedding. Now it's for a funeral instead.

The flowing fabric of the brightly flowered sundress I'm wearing feels as out of place as the wedding dress I rebelliously threatened to wear instead, much to the horror of John's very Catholic family. My usual streamlined black attire would have been more appropriate. But this was supposed to be my day to wear the white gown while celebrating life and love. With this in mind, I had forbidden black at the funeral. Johnny was about light and joy, and I'm determined that today we will celebrate his life despite the despair that threatens to engulf us.

Johnny was born on April 1, an April Fools' baby. I glance around, waiting for him to bound in with his dimpled grin and bouncing curls. The ultimate prank from a man who found the nuances of life endlessly amusing. But instead, the silence lengthens, a darkening shadow covering us all. I am raw, gutted, my chest so tight I can barely breathe. Between the people who pass by to express their sympathy and their personal sadness at the loss of this man beloved by all, I flash out of black despair into indignation and rage. *I'm a bride! Where's my champagne? My joy? My forever?*

I shakily ascend the steps of the church's lectern stage, hug John's godfather, Father Tom, and open my old leather journal to begin my eulogy. I barely hear the words coming out of my mouth over the question spinning through my head: *How am I going to get through this?* A notion—maybe a prayer—rises in my mind, that halfway through reading these words, the same thing that took him from all of us might happen to me. I'll collapse on the floor in a heap, my lungs failing to take in air—respiratory failure. My heart failing to beat—cardiac arrest. In dark agony, my mind pleads with the universe. *Please!* There has to be meaning in this. We all have to make meaning out of this. But that thought only circles back to a crippling, keening *Why?!* The sea of tearful faces comes back into focus. I'd better get this over with while I can. Holding the journal in my trembling hands, I begin.

"Is it possible for a heart to give out because it gave too much? If so, then this is the true cause of Johnny's death."

I lock eyes with Chrissy, one of John's oldest friends, living proof of what I've just said. Only a week ago, John had installed Wi-Fi at her house, along with a collection of laptops he'd refurbished so her children would be set up for success in middle and high school.

"Johnny was a man of magic. He saw the underlying abilities and beauty in people and gave of himself until their beauty shone brightly."

My tearful glance finds Andrea, another dear friend with whom John had spent hours on the phone, encouraging her and providing pivotal support for the critical life changes needed to ensure her and her son's safety.

"A few days ago, I told my dad that John had saved my life. He disagreed and amended my statement to 'John *made* your life.' I agree. John gave me many gifts. He gave *us* so many gifts. Gifts of joy, love, inspiration, integrity, idealism, hope, and so much more. These gifts are now ours to carry with us into the future. To share with others the way Johnny shared them with us."

I see Tim, John's best friend of almost twenty years, sitting front and center. Is it possible that just a few nights ago, the three of us were hanging out, reminiscing and laughing? I flash back to the moment when John interrupted our laughter with a rare display of solemnity to share how much he loved both of us, how important we were to him.

"John made my life. Perhaps in some way he made part of your life. In celebration of this amazing man, I challenge myself and everyone here to take a look at how Johnny impacted us, made a piece of us, and to start living the life he wanted us to have."

I close the journal.

"I love you, Johnny Angel."

Walking away from the lectern, I'm dazed, nauseous. The man who had been my partner for ten years, the man so critical to my being that he felt like the other half of me, is gone. *He is gone.* I try to quell my shaking, keeping one foot moving in front of the next, trying to breathe. Failing. Unbidden, the thought comes to my mind—*Breath, a necessary condition for life.* He had stopped breathing.

My throat catches. It can't be real.

There has to be meaning in this.

Flashes of Memory

The traumatic moments the brain replays with such finely tuned accuracy are known in the scientific community as "flashbulb memories." But to those suffering from posttraumatic stress disorder (PTSD), they feel more like sensory knife cuts that slice into the present moment with what feels like no rhyme or reason. The brain grapples to make sense of these knife cuts and leaves sufferers drowning in deeper and deeper trauma narratives that encompass every possibility missed—what could have been, should have been, but wasn't.

In an instant, the memories can crash into my present. The voice of the 911 operator on the phone, the mad dash to open the gate, the hope still blooming in my chest—*He can still be saved!*—hazy flashes of people coming and going in the apartment, the wooden truth in my chest that my breath kept catching on: that my world would never be the same.

John's niece, ten years old at the time, runs back to the bedroom. I lunge at her, swinging her into my arms and gently holding her in my lap, not wanting her to see what I saw, despite myself, out of the corner of my eye: an EMT grabbing John's foot and dragging him across the floor toward the gurney, covered in a white sheet.

John was supposed to be with his brother Michael, watching basketball or maybe playing video games, while I was supposed to be with Ana, Michael's wife, and John's other sisters and sisters-in-law for a girls' night out.

Only one week later, John and I would have said our vows under an arch of roses, committing to the forever we had promised each other.

But the evening of June 13 took on a life of its own.

**

Ana isn't feeling well, so Michael chooses to stay home with her. John drops me off for the girls' night at his little sister's apartment and then heads home to finalize some last-minute wedding details, work out, and likely spend the rest of the evening indulging in World of Warcraft before picking me up at the Redondo Beach Pier at 10 p.m.

As girls' nights tend to do, especially in this clan, we run long. By 10 p.m., we've just been served our entrées at dinner. When John calls to confirm the predetermined pickup, I respond with words that would forever change my life: "No, honey, it is probably going to be another hour. Can I call you when we're ready to go and let you know where we are?"

The last words we ever exchange are our signature spin on a traditional lovers' sign-off.

Him: "I love you."

Me: "I love you more!"

His laughing rejoinder: "No way!"

Our girls' night revelry continues. As June 13 becomes June 14, I call John to give an update. It goes to voicemail. I call again; his voicemail clicks on again. *He's walking the dogs,* my brain rationalizes, pushing pause on the warning bells that are starting to ring in my mind.

The girls call a cab and we pile in. I try to join their giggling excitement as my rationalizations run like ticker tape in the back of my mind. *People miss calls all the time! This is normal human behavior.* We arrive back at his sister's apartment; the girls open champagne while I call again. Still nothing. My heartbeat picks up speed—something is wrong.

John's sister suggests I stay at her place for the night. Seeing my worry, she gives me a comical eye roll, clearly trying to make me smile. "He probably fell asleep! Typical guy."

By now, though, my intuition is screaming at me at an unignorable decibel. *Something is wrong!* This is not a man who falls asleep on commitments; John has always showed up for me where and when he said he would. Furthermore, I am aware of something his sisters are not: John is very sick.

As yet more champagne emerges from the refrigerator, I wave it off. *I need to leave.* "You're going to be married in a week," they tease. "You're going to spend the rest of your life with him. What's one night?"

But I am starting to shake, my brain and body now electric with fear. I keep repeating, "I have to go. I need to leave, *now.*" I pace, agitated, until my taxi finally arrives.

The usually beautiful ride along the coast from Manhattan Beach to our Playa del Rey apartment feels physically painful. I sit clenched in the back seat, willing the driver to go faster as I call John's phone again and again. *How could he not pick me up? And why isn't he answering? Where is he?!*

In a moment of trauma, the brain encodes the experience less as a narrative and more as a holistic sensory event: everything from the sights and sounds around us to the emotions we feel from one moment to the next. Two core emotions, rage and fear, are coursing through me like white-hot lava, generating irrational and incongruent thoughts. *Maybe he's deep in a World of Warcraft raid and left his phone in the bedroom. Yes. That must be it. Ugh. Jerk!* Yet I know deep inside that something is very, very wrong.

The taxi finally pulls in front of our apartment complex. I fumble with my wallet for a credit card to pay the fare, eventually giving up and shoving into the startled driver's hand the $100 bill John insisted I keep on me in case of emergency. Ironically, my hijacked brain makes way for habit—I sit there, dazed, as he runs a machine and hands me the receipt. Then adrenaline spikes again— *Move, woman!*—and I bolt from the car, leaving the door ajar and waving off the driver as he counts out my change. I fly through the courtyard, scenes from another time flashing in front of my eyes: John's glassy eyes, pupils constricted, gazing listlessly at the ceiling. Nearing our unit, my breath coming in rapid jerks, I strain to see inside the apartment. Lights on, bedroom door closed, and dogs nowhere to be seen.

The front door is locked. Ice-cold fear again escalating, I furiously pound on the door and ring the doorbell. Our dogs' barks light up the night, an outrageous cacophony arising from our apartment, yet . . . nothing. No opening of the bedroom door, no sight of John's dimpled grin and curly hair, no greeting.

Panic sets in. I start kicking at the sliding glass door; the latch is old, and I can break it if I kick hard enough. As I scream his name, the neighbors emerge into the quiet courtyard, likely thinking I've gone insane. One boldly steps into our little patio and threatens to call the police.

"Good! Yes, please!" I shriek.

With a loud snap, the latch finally gives. I yank the door open and bolt to our bedroom. At first, all I see is our jumping dogs. Calling his name, I run around the side of the bed.

What I see will be crystallized into my brain for five years—
what we trauma experts call an intractable and immutably encoded
memory.

There he is.

And I cannot make him breathe.

The next words leave my body as gasps. Expelled. Necessary.
Devastating.

"911, what's your emergency?"

"I think my fiancé is dead."

"Excuse me? Please describe the situation."

"He's cold and he's blue and I cannot make him breathe."

"What's your address?"

For the life of me, I don't know how I am able to recall the
information.

"Are there any gates or barriers to entering the property,
ma'am?"

"There is a gate."

"Go open the gate. A unit is on the way."

"A unit? I need an ambulance. You have to make him breathe."

"Ma'am, go open the gate. They will be there in three to five
minutes."

I run out of the house, yelling at the neighbors still gathered
around our patio to get out of the way. Their previous indignation
and curiosity are now a somber silence punctuated by speculative
whispers. One low comment reaches my ears—"You know the previous tenant's husband died in this unit just a few years ago."

"Shut up!" I bark, throwing open the gate and grabbing a chair
off someone's patio to hold it open.

Breathe, Katy. Breathe. A unit is on the way.

The 911 operator had said it would be three to five minutes.
But it was an eternity, long enough for me to realize what my soul

had already accepted—there was no longer a need to rush. My leaden walk back to the apartment is met with heavy silence from the neighbors crowding the patio. I collapse into a chair at the kitchen table with a view of the open bedroom door in front of me, waiting, horrified, helpless, holding my dogs, no one holding me. I am completely and utterly alone except for, in the next bedroom, the body of the man who was supposed to be my forever.

As the whirling sirens begin to make their presence known, a question cuts through the oppressive darkness: "Do you need to call somebody?" With that simple inquiry, the gravity of the situation slams into me.

I blink.

"Yes?"

No. If I didn't call anyone, then it wouldn't be real. Each day could go on as the others before it. All the people who loved this man so much would be able to wake up on June 14 just as they had on June 13, unless I make a phone call that would forever change everything.

Whom do you call at a moment like this? When the subject is a thirty-two-year-old man a week away from his wedding. A man who had been telling me just this morning how joyous he was about getting married. A man who, the night before, had spent hours discussing his deep gratitude for the relationships he has with me and his best friend, Tim. Whom do you call when that man is dead?

I make a heartbreaking call to Michael, the brother who had been a resounding rock through the entirety of John's life—and who had become one in mine.

After that brief call, I remember only broken pieces. The sirens. The swirling lights. Radios crackling with static. People rushing in, taking action, creating control. They look to me for answers and I stare back at them lost, with ice-cold darkness settling in my gut. *I don't know—he's dead. What do you want me to do? I'm lost.*

It takes a few moments to realize they are assessing whether I had killed him, and whether I have an alibi. This brings forth another layer of agony. *Did I kill him?* Did *I? He collapsed and where was I? With his sisters, having fun. I wasn't here, and now he's dead.*

When they ask where I've been, I hand them the receipt from the taxi; that automatic habit unknowingly created my alibi. Radio crackling, the officer reads the time of my arrival aloud and the emergency medical technicians holler out from the back room that he had likely already been dead thirty to forty-five minutes before I got there. Thirty to forty-five minutes—such a short period, the difference between a cab ride to a Manhattan Beach apartment and one final glass of champagne. The difference between life and death.

While reliving a traumatic moment, the brain is also masterful at finding every possible moment where a different choice could have avoided the disastrous outcome. What if we had kept our regular pickup time and he would have gotten on the road, and what we later learned to be the ultimate cause of his death—respiratory failure—had resulted in a catastrophic car accident? What if our delayed girls' night dinner saved him and others from a car accident that might have taken other lives, perhaps even my life, had I been in the car with him? Hindsight can be a real bitch with its endless hypotheticals; in cognitive behavioral therapy, we call them *counterfactual thinking*. Nevertheless, they are an inherent part of our narrative natures as humans. We will always seek to understand and make meaning.

Oddly, this useless yet compulsive examination of what could have been different is actually a retroactive attempt by the brain to keep us safe. Its primitive logic says that when we know all the eventualities of different possible choices, we can protect ourselves in the future. In the moment, though, it simply feels like a continual replay of all the choices we made—the choices that ultimately resulted in great failure. For me, the failure was in pondering the depth of John's aloneness in his last moment. This was the thought that crystallized into a constant searing agony: *He was alone. I should have been there.*

CHAPTER 2

Tomorrow Begins

"In the transformation from flesh to earth, we see
the symbolic form of transcendence, suggesting its
inevitability whether or not we see it as fit."

—John Sullivan

I return to consciousness in suffocating sunlight. I'm sweating through a heavy duvet, yet a numbness runs through my core. My groggy eyes blink open to find Natalie and Laura, two of my dear friends, sitting with me. Laura's reading a celebrity tabloid, *Star* or *People*—utterly inappropriate for the situation, yet so perfectly irreverent, so endearingly her. I think I actually chuckled, awash with gratitude for their unexpected presence. *Thank God—my people. Who even knew how to reach them?* Then I throw up and return to blissful darkness.

Minutes or hours later, I wake again, anxiety about our beloved dogs (now mine alone) kicking my brain into semi-functionality. "Where's Roscoe and Tinkerbell?" are the first words to reach beyond the echo chamber of my numbness.

Natalie gently pats my arm and points toward a sliding glass door, the epicenter of the searing sunlight in the room. I see the dogs running through the backyard, safe. Relief briefly arrives, chased by another wave of nausea. I promptly throw up again, the biology of shock still in charge. My eyes flutter closed, shutting out the world with the weak comfort of knowing at least one thing is okay. This time, I do not fall back into the escape of sleep. An old coping skill makes its presence known, and I wrap it around me like a beloved childhood blanket—derealization.*

The brain has a remarkable gift for compartmentalizing. In fact, when faced with the horrifying and inescapable experiences we call trauma, the brain can even create its own reality through *dissociation*. When we dissociate, our amygdalae, the tiny brain parts that play a critical role in our survival, create a sense of safety by rerouting the information away from itself. In these moments, we see a decrease in amygdala activity as other brain parts jump online to reduce amygdala engagement, thus mitigating the agonizing experience (Krause-Utz et al., 2017; Lanius et al., 2010).

Those brief moments of numb disconnection were a gift. In the morning after John's death, I hovered just beyond my body, taking stock of the present moment as if through marbled glass. Many years later, my psychologist would ask me how I remember so much about the painful moments of my life. My answer: Do not underestimate the power of the survival brain. For some of us, it is a steel trap for sensory data, cataloging every tiny detail into a complex library of possible future trauma reactions.

---

* According to the American Psychiatric Association's (2013) *Diagnostic and Statistical Manual of Mental Disorders*, derealization is defined as a dissociative symptom that involves a feeling of unreality or a detachment from or unfamiliarity with the world, one's surroundings, or oneself. It is often described as feeling as though one is in a dream or as though the world around oneself is foggy, unreal, or artificial.

Shattered

It is not until late afternoon that I am roused back to consciousness by Ana and my once soon-to-be mother-in-law, Barb, two women who had been bedrocks for safety and connection in the previous years. Behind them, two EMTs stand in the doorway.

Wait, what?

My brain searches for context, flashing the numerous adventures I've had throughout my life that ended with EMTs at the scene. Reality comes crashing in on my blissful dissociation: *John* . . . I recoil against the wall, the duvet now my protective shield from the agonizing memories these uniformed caregivers represent. *Haven't we already been through this? He is dead. They already took him away.*

I feel Barb's soft hand on my arm and Ana's gentle presence seated on my other side.

"Kate, we're worried about you. You're barely breathing. You keep throwing up. We need to make sure you're okay."

I'm delirious but adamant: No no *no!* No hospital for me. I sit up and, once my vitals are assessed, I am declared to be in shock but physically stable. The EMTs leave me to once again collapse into blissful numbness. But this time, reality stays stubbornly present. *This is real.* Every time I close my eyes, I see him—alive and playful, then still and cold. A strobing reel of agony I cannot clear from my brain.

The longest day of my life slowly draws to a close as my parents arrive. I'm ferried from Marina del Rey to our family home in Palm Desert. As my dad's car carves its graceful way across the California desert, I sit stoically in the back seat. The deep, black desert sky yawns open above us. A snippet of a quote from Ralph

Waldo Emerson creeps into my mind: "Let us advance on Chaos and the Dark."

***

We pull into my parents' garage to the sound of the phone ringing inside the house. My mother rushes to answer it as my dad carefully eases me out of the car. Walking in the door, we hear my mom on the phone, offering to whomever is on the other end a litany of warnings not to come to the house that night. "Please do not bring Nana Kay here. Katy's going to bed. She can barely stand and needs to sleep. It's dark outside. It's not safe—the ground is too unsteady. Come tomorrow."

Her words go unheeded; my aunt and my grandmother arrive shortly thereafter. It's pitch black out, the house smothered in the darkness of the surrounding mountains, nothing but starlight to guide the way. With no one anticipating their arrival, my grandmother, Nana Kay, exits the car without assistance. She slips. She falls. She breaks her hip.

I find Nana Kay sitting on the cool concrete of the street curb, her face twisted in pain. Kneeling down beside her, I can feel my brain once again warring with the shocking, surreal quality of the situation. *How can this possibly be real? How is any of this real?* In the vast desert sky, the stars glow like beacons above us, shining with an ageless wisdom that our temporal human spirits will never grasp.

Despite her own pain, Nana Kay squeezes my hand with gentle yet firm assurance. Her resolve and strength are tangible, a grounding force in the pain swirling around us. She is telling me—lecturing me, actually—in her inimitable way: "You are one of the strongest women I have ever met. You will get through this."

I stare at her.

"You're sitting there with a shattered hip, and you're telling me this?!" The half-laugh in my words ends with my voice breaking. "How did you survive when Boppie died?"

Boppie, as the deeply revered Charles Augustus Truitt was known to his grandchildren, was her world. Theirs was indeed a love for the ages.

She answers, "Honey, it gets softer, and you will carry him with you."

We hear the wailing ambulance growing closer, the flashing lights throwing an eerie glow across the black desert landscape. I lean over, head between my legs, fighting the urge to panic, vomit, or both. For a moment, Nana Kay's hand rests gently on my back.

"Go," she tells me. Then she squeezes my hand again and tells me with strength and knowingness that radiates from her core, "I love you, and I love John, and John is here with us."

I leave her sitting there on that curb, not knowing it would be the beginning of Nana's decline and eventual death, just four months later. She would tell me later that this was the moment where her spirit quietly whispered, "Enough—it is time to go be with Charlie, my love."

**

That first night and the following week are a blur, punctuated with mere flashes of images rather than full memories. The desolate aloneness, the nausea, the disbelief, the constant waiting for John to walk into the room. For those sparkling eyes, dimpled cheeks, and his impish grin to make their appearance.

However, even in the deepest darkness, there can luckily be light. Although the brain remembers the dark moments more powerfully (Rozin & Royzman, 2001), I'm continually grateful for the brief flashes of positive memories that surface as well. The amygdala plays a crucial role in encoding both the brilliant and the horrifying (Cunningham & Brosch, 2012; Cunningham & Kirkland, 2013; Guex et al., 2020; Hamann et al., 1999).

One of those flashes is a slow journey to the kitchen that stops short when I hear my mom calling every single one of our friends near and far to tell them that the wedding was off, that John was gone. I collapse into a chair and rest my forehead on the cool surface of her dining room table. For a long time, she doesn't know I'm there. She paces between two sets of large sliding glass doors as she repeats the horror of the past two days over and over, one call after another. Her voice never falters. When she does finally take note of my presence, she brings me a glass of water and gently rests her hand on my back. A quiet connection. A reminder: "I'm here. You're not alone."

Tears begin gently coursing down my cheeks, the sobs of anguish temporarily exhausted and the tidal waves of what was to come still unknown. Achingly I silently marvel at my powerhouse mother. *God, how strong is she to have just lost a son?* For ten years, that's what John had been to her. She had embraced him and all his quirky delightfulness from the very beginning. Now she is spending hours calling person after person—who just a day prior were planning on joining us for a beautiful garden wedding in Santa Barbara—to instead tell them, "Here's the funeral information if you would like to come, and yes, we understand if you can't make it." What a terrible task for a woman beset with her own grief, let alone tying up all the loose ends into perfect bows in the face of a grenade that had decimated her daughter's world.

She would later tell me that she barely slept in the weeks following John's death. Several times each night, she would tiptoe into my room and rest her hand on my chest, ensuring its quiet rise and fall, terrified I would stop breathing as suddenly as he had.

Roses and Remembrance

After a few days, we drive back to Michael and Ana's house. The funeral is waiting for us. It starts with the particularly brutal experience of returning to that dreaded apartment, tasked with selecting objects for John's casket and choosing his funeral attire—a surreal exercise, contemplating what he would treasure as he embarks on his passage into the afterlife.

On the drive over, John's sister Amelia and their nephew Nicky attempt to lighten the mood by recapping the top hits of Johnny's prankster stories and playing songs from his punk rock playlist. We cheekily yell the lyrics from John's favorite punk bands out the car windows as we drive. But despite my best attempt to distract myself from the task at hand, it's near impossible for me to quell my rising nausea, especially once we round the corner onto our street. I spy the courtyard gate, whose resounding clank affirmed the bitter truth—*he was gone.* The heaviness of that leaden walk back to the apartment filled me all over again.

Trauma doesn't just ravage the mind. As renowned traumatologist Bessel van der Kolk (2014) reminds us in his seminal book *The Body Keeps the Score,* the body carries the imprint of the agony we've experienced just as vibrantly as the memories inside the mind. The brain links into all the sensations besieging the body—what we're seeing, hearing, smelling, tasting, and touching—as well as the emotions flowing through us. These thoughts, body responses, and emotions come together to build the sensory narrative of the trauma. From that moment on, this sensory narrative remains in the brain, ready to hijack the mind and body at a moment's notice if similar stimuli should appear in the future (Ruden, 2011).

Just as my mind and body are about to take flight into trauma-driven panic, I feel Amelia's gentle hand upon mine, her tenderness penetrating the tornado of emotions that threaten to overwhelm me.

"You don't have to go in, honey," she says lovingly.

Tears spring to my eyes, knowing her own agony. She and John had been inseparable since his birth; in their family of six, she was his soul sister. I glance in the rearview mirror and catch Nicky's gaze; he nods in agreement. I release a heavy sigh and give them a pained smile, grateful for their support and understanding in the face of their own incredible loss.

"No, we are all in this together. He was our person."

I reach back and grab Nicky's hand. We *are* all in this together. In grief, the journeys are different but the way the brain grapples to make sense of the loss is the same for all. With a brave glance shared among the three of us, we exit the car.

A rose, bright red, lies on the concrete curb just a foot from where my foot touches the pavement. An AOL Instant Messenger conversation from early in our relationship intrudes into my mind:

Femme484 (me): I found another rose under my left tire. Any idea?

Conn3x (John): A guardian angel. Your tire needs air BTW.

Femme484: Ah. A purposeful rose.

Conn3x: Many purposes. But safety first, I have big plans for us.

I met John during my college freshman orientation in 1999. We forged a friendship, a connection that quickly took on an unexpected life of its own. His courting began with leaving red roses for me where I would least expect to find them. There were hundreds of roses over the years, always unexpected, always important.

Tears well up, threatening to overflow unbidden as my mind flashes back to a sign-off in an email John sent me just a few weeks ago: *Here's to our rose garden Katy, my love for you is so pure. Keep me in your thoughts, in your heart, because that's where I'm keeping you.*

Human lives are intricately woven together by the stories we tell ourselves and share with others. Within us, there resides a profound desire to find meaning, to make sense of the intricate tapestry of our lives and the relationships we hold dear. Foundationally, we are meaning-making beings, and it is through the sharing of stories, the preservation of cherished memories, and the imparting of wisdom that we understand the world around us. In times of loss, these stories become our guiding lights, offering solace and connection, providing the meaning we seek. Our brains, in the aftermath of grief and trauma, become finely attuned to the meaning-making process, amplifying the importance of everyday experiences.

In the following weeks, months, and years, I would find many single roses. These became gentle—and at times lifesaving—reminders that he was still with me and that there must be a larger meaning. Within the dark unknowingness of the future, they empowered me to put one foot in front of the other in the face of grief and PTSD that left me completely rudderless. After all, what do you do in the days after your life ends? Even after studying the intricacies of trauma for ten years, I didn't have an answer. All I had were thousands of text messages from John with the mantra "There are bigger plans." What were those plans? With my future burned into ash, without him beside me to believe in what I could not, what hope was there for thriving? How could I hope to do anything better than survive? All I knew was that the first step must be to keep breathing.

CHAPTER 3

Patterns

"Humans don't survive alone in nature; they die—and as a result, we are all hardwired to belong to groups. But the only way to guarantee membership in a group is to be needed by it, so being unneeded can feel catastrophic."

—Sebastian Junger

Like the unique chemical bonds that occur between different elements, the cocreated relationship between two people is always one of a kind. The loves, the losses, and the stories and patterns of past life experiences all play out within this partnership. Our nervous systems align so that we intuit each other in ways others cannot begin to know. Our partner's knowing glance and sway in their walk, a quirk of an eyebrow or clench of a jaw, send signals to us that we may not even be consciously aware of. We mirror each other, creating an endless circle of seeing and being seen, knowing and being known.

This is why losing a partner can feel like losing a part of ourselves. This is what happened with John and me. We were so commingled with each other—John and Kate, Kate and John— that it felt as though one wouldn't exist without the other.

This type of attachment in a relationship may not sound the healthiest. Frankly, it's not. We started dating when I was nineteen and John was only eighteen months older. Our brains were not even fully formed at this time (Arain et al., 2013; Giedd et al., 1999).

Both of us carried scars from painful childhood experiences and had similarly struggled with the effects of anxiety, depression, and attention deficit hyperactivity disorder (ADHD) throughout our childhoods. My past taught me self-preservation through solitude, yet I longed for genuine connection. John's upbringing pushed him to stay ahead of chaos, rescuing others while silently seeking salvation himself. Our unique survival instincts and developmental experiences of our youth merged and became puzzle pieces that completed one another—a union blending laughter, love, and joy while also healing deeply rooted patterns shaped by adverse childhood experiences (ACEs) we faced before turning eighteen.

Adverse Childhood Experiences

In the late 1990s, the world of mental health was forever changed by a now-famous study on the long-term health impacts of ACEs. These may include enduring emotional, physical, or sexual abuse, witnessing domestic violence, having a family member who struggles with substance abuse, experiencing neglect, and so much more. Conducted by Kaiser Permanente and the Centers for Disease Control and Prevention (CDC), this groundbreaking study validated something many people already knew from painful personal experience: The events of our childhood are far more impactful to us than meets the eye (Felliti et al., 1998; Burke Harris, 2014). Since that original study, additional research from the CDC (2019) has found that 61 percent of the population has experienced at least one ACE, while 16 percent has experienced four or more.

ACEs not only cast a long shadow over our formative years but also wield a lasting influence on our adult lives. They propel us into a precarious realm of heightened vulnerability where the odds stack against us, increasing the likelihood of chronic conditions in adulthood, from cardiovascular disease, stroke, and cancer to asthma, chronic obstructive pulmonary disease, kidney disease, diabetes, and the burden of overweight or obesity. Sadly, the impact doesn't stop with health adversities. ACEs also infiltrate our emotional well-being, taking a toll on mental health and leading us toward an assortment of risky health behaviors (Merrick et al., 2019; Nelson et al., 2020; Suglia et al., 2018). The likelihood of smoking and alcohol use is also increased significantly, with those reporting four or more ACEs being twice as likely to smoke or use large amounts of alcohol and six times as likely to engage in drinking behavior that negatively impacts their lives (Hughes et al., 2017). The odds of opioid abuse are three times higher for individuals who have four or more ACEs (Quinn et al., 2016), and the risk of engaging in suicidal behavior is thirty times higher (Hughes et al., 2017). In short, if you have struggled or are struggling in the wake of your own ACEs, please know that you, like John and me, are not alone.

As our intertwined relationship developed, John and I cocreated a world where we could step into our inner darkness, exist in our rawest forms of pained vulnerability, and create something new. I made a world for him where he was able to have agency and impact, where he mattered beyond his charm and intelligence. In turn, he created a world for me where I was able to experience the feeling of being connected, safe, and seen. It was as though finally, after nineteen long years, I could breathe.

On one hand, this interwoven development made us closer in a few months than some couples get in a lifetime. On the other hand, in building a foundation of Self that depended upon one another for a felt sense of safety, we'd unwittingly created a relationship doomed for disaster if something ever happened to the other.

Building the Core Values of Survival

Our brains love to find and follow patterns. They run our lives even without our conscious awareness. If you like chocolate and you're hungry (and maybe even if you're *not* hungry), when someone asks you if you want some chocolate, you will likely say yes even if you've never previously had the particular chocolate in question. You do not know for sure that you will like that particular chocolate, yet the brain rapidly says *I know I like chocolate, so yes, I want this chocolate.* From our very first breath, we begin building our own instruction manuals for life based on these patterns, guides for how we will live and whom we believe ourselves to be.

Our brains also develop patterns around relationships but at a more nuanced level. The brain feels safety from having familiar patterns repeated or completed, so much so that it will even push us into punishing and abusive experiences to continue or reconcile patterns from our pasts.

These patterns develop from life experiences. We have three core principles or values for survival that are critical in guiding our development of Self, or whom we experience ourselves to be in the world and how we experience the world around us (Cunningham & Brosch, 2012; Truitt, 2022). These three core values for survival are best expressed as questions:

How do I stay safe?

How can I belong and be lovable?

How am I successful?

From the time we are born, our brains are exploring, learning, and developing our unique understandings of these critical values. While the development continues throughout our lives, the most impactful experiences are our earliest ones, and primarily those within our community and concerning the teachings of our caregivers. It doesn't matter whether we are talking about today or 20,000 years ago—a two-year-old, a seven-year-old, and an eleven-year-old all need a community around them. It isn't easy at those younger ages to survive without one. Indeed, humans generally are not very good at surviving on their own—they do best with a village. This is why our brains are naturally primed to notice and be concerned about what others think and feel about us.

As children, we learn by exploring. I help a friend and am praised—*I am helpful!* I hit my friend when they take my toy and I get scolded—*I am bad.* (Or, hopefully, with kind and loving context from the caregiver who gave the correction, *That behavior was bad*).

ACEs can significantly impact how our brains start developing their core values for survival. Growing up, I was chronically ill. Many forms of physical pain plagued my young body, but my survival brain quickly identified that my physical symptoms caused stress to my family. My developing brain perceived this stress as being burdensome to my family, and so the Self-identifying ideas of *I am sick, I am a burden, I cause stress* began creeping through my brain. My older sister gathered the bulk of the family's limited attention, playing out her own survival needs while building her sense of Self. My dad was hard-driving, the product of a "pull yourself up by the bootstraps" ideology. My mom was the backbone of our family unit. Beautiful, intelligent, and no-nonsense, she held us together. My parents both worked tirelessly to give their daughters more than they had in their childhoods. Still, like many latchkey households of the 1980s, our ineptitude for expressing feelings made our family disconnected from each other, physically and emotionally.

The Self that we become is defined not only by our own experiences but also by the learned experiences of our caregivers. As an adult, I have learned more about my parents' childhoods and notice that my childhood was nearly a reproduction of theirs, particularly when it came to relationships and emotional connection. Following the patterns of their upbringing (and their own ACEs), my parents instilled a fundamental concept in my sister and me: We must always be "fine." In family relationships as well as in the world, no matter how badly we might be suffering, we must never make our problems someone else's problem.

As an adult, I understand how this happened. But as a child, there was no context. This was simply the norm. Like any child, all I had was my evolving brain and body. And boy, did they do an excellent job of learning how to help me survive.

All the way up to early adulthood, our brains are learning what works and doesn't work; the neural pathways of the Self are being built all the time, in every experience. But once we hit adolescence, a specific process called *synaptic pruning* ramps up. In this process, the thinking areas of our brains begin prioritizing what information they need to keep while clearing out the rest. Like a snake shedding its skin, the brain leaves behind what it no longer needs to stay alive while the essential Self remains. We start learning more about who we are supposed to be while linking deeply into the core survival principles we've developed, turning them from questions into statements:

I stay safe by . . . .

I can belong and be lovable if . . .

I can be successful when . . .

What the brain learns about these core values for Self can be positive, negative, and anything in between. One person might learn to stay safe by being kind, bold, and loving while another stays safe by being aggressive, by dissociating and disconnecting, by being defensive or by shutting down. Some of my own foundational core values included:

> *I stay safe by disconnecting from myself and by pleasing others.*
>
> *I can belong and be lovable if I do not need anything from others and am not being burdensome.*
>
> *I can be successful when I deal with my problems—I only rely on myself.*

Synaptic pruning takes place all the way through adolescence (from approximately ages ten to seventeen) to our emerging adulthood (approximately ages eighteen to twenty-nine). All the while, our brains are solidifying our sense of Self. By adulthood, our brains essentially say, *I've explored, I've learned, and this is who I am and how I live life.* The conclusions of adolescence are experienced as unnuanced facts about who we are:

I am (un)safe.

I am (un)lovable.

I am (un)successful.

This is how our core values—seeded at an early age, often before we are even aware of them—guide how we behave, make decisions, build relationships, think about the world, and much more.

Survival Values at Work:
The Side Effects of Being "Fine"

I began puberty at age nine, which made for a brutal summer between third and fourth grade. It was as though I went from being "too tall but cute" to large, hairy, and oily overnight. Severe acne plastered itself across my young face, my feet rapidly grew to a size 10, and my clothes became uncomfortably tight and ridiculously short. Hormones, the biological warfare of adolescence, had begun to wreak havoc in both my internal and external worlds. I was not prepared for any of it.

In addition to the usual trials and tribulations of puberty, there was another factor at play for me, one that is heartbreakingly common for many children: I had a bully. Research from the U.S. Department of Education (2019) highlights that one in five people experience bullying as a child. My bully regularly physically, emotionally, and verbally assaulted me. She came in the form of a close family friend, a girl near my own age, who I am intentionally leaving unnamed here. She had already been my personal tormentor for years, but puberty gave her a whole new set of ammunition. I was the brunt of her endless vicious jokes—nothing was too big or too small to be exploited. I quickly learned that not only was my body a vessel of pain, but it was also embarrassing, socially unacceptable, and something to be constantly and critically scrutinized.

It is probably not surprising that debilitating depression and social anxiety began slinking into the corners of my mind. By age ten, I'd begun daydreaming about going to sleep and never waking up. I remember my bully telling me more times than I can count that I should go kill myself, that it would make everyone happy, and I was haunted by wondering whether that would work—if it would offer an escape from the pain, if it was really the only way I could stop being the burden I believed I was. It was not until a few years later that, when reading a Christopher Pike book, I would finally have a name for this strange phenomenon in my mind: suicidal thoughts.

You can imagine how my pain and anxiety disrupted the family, causing stress on a system that seemed already stretched to its limit. Knowing that I was defying the unwritten family rule of "be fine," my adaptable little brain had to learn a new way of surviving. That's when I started to be quiet. I could not "be fine" if people knew how I was suffering, so I worked hard to silence my voice. Instead, I aimed for overachievement in the hope of preemptively making up for my inevitable missteps. This protected me in the short term, but in the long term, it was devastating—a perfect case study of the counterintuitive way that these survival patterns show up. Silencing turned into numbing, and before long, I learned how to dissociate, a tool that served my brain well in the coming years, even if it is not a preferable long-term way to exist in the world.

The core of the problem was that the threats to my physical, emotional, and psychological safety came from within my family, my community, even from within my own body. In particular, because my bully was from within our close community, it was difficult for my family to see the abuse for what it was and to respond appropriately. There were times I would stand up to the bully, but the repercussions of increased harm quickly taught me to stay quiet. On the rare occasion when I was able to break through my self-imposed silence and ask for help from the adults in my life, I received messages that I needed to handle it on my own or simply steer clear of her, an impossible task. My little brain concluded there was no point in standing up for myself and that no one was going to do it for me either.

My core values for survival were being shaped, and my brain built a powerful framework for survival: I was alone, and to stay safe, I either needed to adjust my inner life to accept that being alone and on my own was true, or if that was too painful, I could end my life altogether. Of course, I now know that no adolescent can be so disgusting that they should die. But to my young Self, it was my own existence that I started to see as a threat. Even here, you can see the loving yet heartbreakingly counterintuitive ways our brains make sense of the world to help us survive. When I look back at the photos of myself during this time, I can see that there is no way my footsteps could make an entire room shake, despite the fact that each time I walked into a room, she and her friends would start taunting me: "Boom bada boom, boom bada boom! Katy, you're making the entire room shake. Get out of here! You're so fat! You're going to make the floor collapse!" But at the time, I didn't know these things. I just knew that all the girls and boys, even my own friends, would dissolve into giggles and pick up her catchy chant. It followed me around school and began to resonate in my soul.

Children can be cruel, especially children who are themselves hurting, and I now believe the bully was also in her own version of deep pain. But eventually, like many other people who experience severe bullying, I began to believe that I indeed *was* the horrible things that were said to me and about me. This was another of my brain's survival strategies: If I bought into those labels, maybe I would be safe. They felt terrible, but at least I would be in alignment with the person who was bigger, stronger, and more powerful than me and also with what my community was inadvertently teaching me.

When I was around twelve, my mother took note of my severe social anxiety and deeply rooted insecurities. Given our family's paramount value for being "fine," she sidestepped the emotional part and instead set about fixing what she perceived to be the problem by putting me on the acne medicine Accutane* and, once my acne cleared about a year later, signing me up for modeling classes.

In retrospect, I see the reasoning behind her decision—modeling would teach me poise, presence, maybe even confidence, but you can imagine the terror the idea of modeling would bring to a teenager beset by depression, social anxiety, and body dysmorphia. Still, part of me thought perhaps this was a new step forward toward increasing my value in my family's eyes, thus securing the safety, belonging, lovability, and success I'd all but given up on.

As I began modeling, I was stunned to learn that my body and my face were not the atrocities that my bully had made me believe they were. I started to book modeling jobs and was given new forms of satisfying those core values for survival. Carving my body into the "heroin chic" ideal of the mid-1990s became a new focus for how I could be lovable, belong, and stay successful. I now had a version of worth that was achievable for me, and my teenage brain was ecstatic—*I'll take it!*

Modeling would eventually take me to Los Angeles, and I was lucky to receive a scholarship to Loyola Marymount University. And so it was that a terrified eighteen-year-old girl landed in L.A.,

---

* Since 2000, Accutane (generically known as isotretinoin) has been the center of an ongoing investigation regarding an increased risk of suicidal thoughts and acts of completed suicide (for review, see Gieler & Gieler, 2020). If you are taking Accutane and notice changes in your mood or experience thoughts of suicide, please contact your physician and/or a suicide helpline. Visit www.findahelpline .com for a global list of helplines.

full of false bravado and a vacant soul, having learned the way to survive is to be fine, be silent, be whatever people need you to be.

The Power of Being Seen

My friendship with John began during my first weeks of living in Los Angeles. I was definitely out of my league in that city; even driving on the streets was terrifying. I was good at false bravado though. By that time, I had become a talented people pleaser and perfectionist, skilled at using performance and achievement to hide the pain I carried from not only years of illness and bullying but also multiple sexual assaults and an eating disorder that would eventually land me in the hospital with severe cardiac arrhythmia and at significant risk of having a heart attack. Having been taught that exploring or expressing my emotions could lead to trouble, my brain kept me emotionally disconnected from the world around me. I learned to square my shoulders, hold my head up tall, and follow the mantra *fake it 'til you make it*, all to cover the deeply rooted existential angst about my value and worth.

A few weeks after I met John, he invited me to go to a party with some of his old high school friends. College students are not exactly known for their networking skills. As we walked in, the group melted into the crowd to greet their friends, leaving me stranded in a corner—a master class in looking cool while battling the relentless rise of panic that always haunted me in social situations. At one point, John looked over at me and seemed to assess my emotional state on a deeper level. He walked over and declared a little too loudly, "You look like you need some attention."

Burning red shame crept up my cheeks. I glanced around quickly to see if anyone had heard, mortified to be called out so completely.

I did not need attention. (Yes, I did.)

I did not want attention. (Yes, I did.)

I definitely did not want to be noticed while embarrassingly alone. How dare he!

John's eyes were kind, and a playful energy danced across his face. "You're used to being the center of attention, aren't you?"

I couldn't help but laugh—scoff, actually—at that statement. I shook my head no. "Absolutely not."

He leaned back, seemingly taking stock of me. He didn't know me very well at this point, and most of our exchanges had been simple playful barbs. I was good at keeping people at arm's length, but I could feel my cheeks turning a brighter red under the spotlight of his caring attention, something I both longed for and was terrified of.

My search for an easy escape was interrupted by his gentle hand on my arm. "Hey, can I get you something?"

Spying the keg outside, I cocked my head in that direction. "Beer?"

"Atta girl!" he grinned, and motioned for me to join him and his friends standing around the keg.

Later, he would tell me that I reminded him in that moment of a scared kitten, ready to pounce or to run, but perhaps just wanting love. It was the birth of his future nickname for me: Kitten.

That exchange planted the seed of what would become our relationship. Each of us presented an unexpected anomaly to the survival values life had taught our brains to follow. We fulfilled the patterns of what should have been in our childhoods, and we reveled in finally being seen and heard in a safe space with a safe other, in meeting parts of each other that nobody else ever had.

Take a Breath and Create Possibilities

When I met John, I had no sense of hope or possibility. I did not seek opportunities to thrive. I was resistant to and avoidant of human connection, deeply cynical of the notion that humans would go out of their way in service of one another. Amid my frequent debates with John about the innate biological need for human connection, I would often press my point by singing the words of Simon and Garfunkel: "I am a rock, I am an island." It's hard to argue with the greats.

Each debate always ended the exact same way: with John shining a light on the inner strengths and abilities we all held. He believed that humans are incredibly beautiful in their rawness and, at the same time, completely capable of coming together for the creation of awesome and important change. Little by little, his narrative soaked through my cynicism and became a shining beacon of the possibilities available to everyone. He saw in me something larger than I could see in myself. He embraced my possibilities and believed in me when my mind and body were trying to self-destruct. In many ways, he was the surrogate for my Self, providing a different outcome to several old survival patterns in my brain:

I wanted to shrink and fade into the background. John's words echoed with reassurance: *"I see you."*

I was terrified of rejection and felt out of control in a dangerous world. John became a soothing refuge: *"You are safe with me."*

I lived my days in ruminating cycles of shame and struggled to find my value and worth. John's unwavering support whispered, *"I believe in you."*

* * *

Twelve days after John's death, my pen returned to my faithful leather journal. Just a few pages after his eulogy, I scrawled this on tear-stained pages:

June 25th, 2009

So, what happens now? I currently reside in a world of avoidance and anguish. I want so badly for this not to be real. How can it be real?! This is not our life. I don't know what life is. What this life is. If it was "his" time, why couldn't it have also been my time? Death? Something? Anything other than what this is? I didn't die. Johnny helped pull me out.

The haunting question persisted, "*Why? There must be meaning in this.*" The pain of losing John continued to intensify. In our ten years together, he had become the foundation from which I drew the strength to recover from the wounds of my past. His presence was a steady beacon of hope during my journey out of the consuming darkness that haunted me since childhood.

He taught me how to love myself. Then he died, and my foundation dropped out from underneath me. After studying trauma for almost ten years, I slammed right into the hubris of my two bachelor's degrees, two master's degrees, and nearly completed doctorate. I thought I knew so much. In reality, I knew very little. I was suddenly eighteen years old again, lost again in that black hole of despairing aloneness.

If I was ever going to journey back from this new nightmarish reality to a place where I was surviving, recovering, and ultimately thriving, I would need to somehow break those old patterns on my own. I would have to create my own foundation based on a new empowered version of my Self. That would mean confronting some hard truths and scary emotions along the way. I was not sure I knew how to do that.

CHAPTER 4

Ready or Not, Here We Go

"Trauma is not what happens to you
but what happens inside you."

—Gabor Maté

A s is all too human, my first attempt to "get over" the grief and trauma means returning to the survival patterns of my developmental years: function and perform, numb and disconnect. Diving back into work keeps my mind occupied. An avid Aikido student, I return to my dojo. Each day, at least while the sun shines, I somehow keep breathing. But each night, when the sun sets, a few friends gather in my home to hold a not-so-subtle vigil over my exhausted soul. The weight of being left behind is suffocating, making me yearn to stop the world and get off. Suddenly this poem, written many years prior, is once again my daily emotional reality:

So here I climb through this darkened hole
to find an abyss waiting for me.
Screaming out to my silenced ears,
lost words forgotten in yesterday's memory
and tales told forever in the past.

I glance and dance,
along that broken cliff,
skimming the moans and sighs of the abyss and wander . . .
alone.

With sweeping arms and fluttering lashes,
I swirl and sway along that perimeter
until one toe slips,
one finger misses a syllable
and I collapse,
into the oblivion . . .

—Kate Truitt, 2001

During my therapeutic recovery journey in my twenties, I had built new patterns and found healthy strategies for survival. But nothing had prepared me for the reawakening of experiences in my mind and body that I thought were no longer a part of my life—dissociation, depression, and more. Once again, I am dreaming of a collapse into oblivion.

Grief happens both in our heads and our hearts. It affects our physiology and neurobiology. We can know in our heads what is happening, but the ability to heal hinges on our heart's ability to embrace and process the loss. While I could rely on many years of education to help my head explain what was happening to me, I could not make my heart or soul move forward.

For example, my head is aware that in the weeks following John's death, I definitely met the diagnostic criteria for acute stress disorder (American Psychiatric Association [APA], 2013).

Acute Stress Disorder: Code 308.3

A. Exposure to actual or threatened death, serious injury, or sexual violation in one (or more) of the following ways:

  1. Directly experiencing the traumatic event(s). – *Check!*

  2. Witnessing, in person, the events(s) as it occurred to others. – *Check!*

  3. Learning that the events(s) occurred to a close family member or close friend. Note: In cases of actual or threatened death of a family member or friend, the events(s) must have been violent or accidental. – *Check!*

  4. Experiencing repeated or extreme exposure to aversive details of the traumatic event(s) (e.g., first responders collecting human remains, police officers repeatedly exposed to details of child abuse). – *Check!*

B. Presence of nine (or more) of the following symptoms from any of the five categories of intrusion, negative mood, dissociation, avoidance, and arousal beginning or worsening after the traumatic event(s) occurred:

Intrusion Symptoms

  1. Recurrent, involuntary, and intrusive distressing memories of the traumatic event(s). – *Not yet*

  2. Recurrent distressing dreams in which the content and/or affect of the dream are related to the event(s). – *Check!*

  3. Dissociative reactions (e.g., flashbacks) in which the individual feels or acts as if the traumatic event(s) were

recurring. (Such reactions may occur on a continuum, with the most extreme expression being a complete loss of awareness of present surroundings.) – *Not yet*

4. Intense or prolonged psychological distress or marked physiological reactions in response to internal or external cues that symbolize or resemble an aspect of the traumatic event(s) – *Check!*

Negative Mood

5. Persistent inability to experience positive emotions (e.g., inability to experience happiness, satisfaction, or loving feelings). – *Check!*

Dissociative Symptoms

6. An altered sense of the reality of one's surroundings or oneself (e.g., seeing oneself from another's perspective, being in a daze, time slowing). – *Check!*

7. Inability to remember an important aspect of the traumatic event(s) (typically due to dissociative amnesia and not to other factors such as head injury, alcohol, or drugs). – *I wish!*

Avoidance Symptoms

8. Efforts to avoid distressing memories, thoughts, or feelings about or closely associated with the traumatic event(s). – *Check!*

9. Efforts to avoid external reminders (people, places, conversations, activities, objects, situations) that arouse

distressing memories, thoughts, or feelings about or closely associated with the traumatic event(s). – *Check!*

Arousal Symptoms

10. Sleep disturbance (e.g., difficulty falling or staying asleep, restless sleep). – *Check!*

11. Irritable behavior and angry outbursts (with little or no provocation), typically expressed as verbal or physical aggression toward people or objects. – *Nope*

12. Hypervigilance. – *Not yet*

13. Problems with concentration. – *Check!*

14. Exaggerated startle response. – *Always and check!*

C. Duration of the disturbance (symptoms in Criterion B) is 3 days to 1 month after trauma exposure. – *Check!*

D. The disturbance causes clinically significant distress or impairment in social, occupational, or other important areas of functioning. – *Check!*

E. The disturbance is not attributable to the physiological effects of a substance (e.g., medication or alcohol) or another medical condition (e.g., mild traumatic brain injury) and is not better explained by brief psychotic disorder. – *Check!*

But meanwhile, my heart and soul can't muster the will to get the help my head tells me I need. If anything, acknowledging the need for help freaks me out, ironically reinforcing the idea that I am weak and out of control. My old survival patterns of finding strength in being alone run fast and true. Plus, I am a therapist. I

understand what is happening in my brain. I shouldn't need help—
right? (Wrong.) Falling back into the comfort of isolation feels safer
than reaching out for support.

A couple of weeks after John's death, a colleague with whom
I had worked on the hospice wing at the Veteran Affairs Medical
Center contacts me with a kind message: "Make sure you're giving
yourself the support you need. You have to feel. You must mourn."

Mourning is the outward expression of the deep sorrow we feel.
It is an important part of how we share our emotional experiences
of loss with the world around us. Ideally, an honest expression of
mourning creates connection with others who have also experienced loneliness and loss.

For me, however, having learned as a child that I was alone
with my emotions, expressing the depth of my pain and engaging
in conscious mourning simply doesn't occur to me. In fact, as a veteran trauma survivor, I am actually pretty proud of how well my
brain is holding up. I'm forgetting that the more traumatic experiences we have in our pasts, the more vulnerable our brains and
bodies are to intensified reactions to new traumatic experiences.
My brain is not just any old human brain experiencing that devastating night. My brain is prolific with risk factors: a high number
of ACEs, a history of traumatic events, and of course, a history of
psychiatric disorders—my anxiety and depression played a major
role in my developmental experience (Breslau, 2001; Brewin et al.,
2000; McLaughlin et al., 2013; Ozer et al., 2003; Sareen, 2014).
Even while my brain is paying attention to data points that could
help me "pull myself up by the bootstraps," my old survival patterns are lurking in the shadows, waiting for their cue.

As a result, when I'm not in the throes of acute stress symptoms,
I am in the state of perpetual dissociative disconnection from my

emotions. Dr. Mardi Horowitz (2011) describes this as "benumbed": feeling surrounded by a layer of cotton or insulation. Frankly, being "benumbed" is nice. It feels as though my brain and body hold a meeting in which I, the conscious entity known as Kate, am not invited. In this meeting, it is decided that our old survival pal *dissociation* is the best candidate to lead us into the unknown future (Dalgleish & Power, 2004; Sierra & Berrios, 1998).

Using old patterns to deal with new things will only work for so long. To others, my dissociated state looks like strength; I am congratulated for my ability to "keep it together." In truth, it leaves me even more vulnerable to the eventual onset of complex grief and posttraumatic stress disorder. With more and more friends voicing their concern about my odd sleeping patterns and disjointed emotional presentation, I eventually acknowledge that I need help. I need to see a therapist.

***

As I park my car behind the ancient Tudor home that houses Dr. Blue's office suite, I pause for a moment to collect my thoughts. I know from both personal and professional experience that therapy is a unique experience, requiring immediate transparency and vulnerability with a complete stranger. I have "tried on" many therapists in my own healing journey, and my psychiatrist, Dr. Blue, has been a continual presence throughout my graduate career. She was the first one to identify and successfully treat the previously undiagnosed ADHD that had played a major role in some of my early life difficulties, and with her guidance and support, I'd been able to shed the majority of psychotropic medications that had kept me functioning throughout my undergraduate career. Upon hearing my heartbreaking news, she refers me to a colleague who practices across the hall from her office, specializing in traumatic grief and loss.

As I enter the foyer, the receptionist stops me. When I share that I am here to see Therapist X* instead of Dr. Blue, she tells me to take a seat in a wooden chair next to her desk, a sharp contrast to my usual comforting experience of being waved up the stairs to Dr. Blue's private waiting room.

The minutes tick by with no notification from Therapist X. The foyer isn't private by any means, and I feel even more discombobulated by the people coming and going. By the time Therapist X finally emerges to greet me, it's about fifteen minutes into my session time. She invites me upstairs, motions for me to sit on the sofa and, as we both get settled, asks, "So what brings you in today?"

I know my face registers shock. I spoke to her on the phone just two days ago, giving her details that would tend to be memorable to most people: finding my fiancé dead one week prior to our wedding and not being able to resuscitate him, the wedding turned funeral, referral from her colleague across the hall. But she doesn't seem to remember. Starting to feel a little queasy, I review those details again, watching her face for some glimmer of recognition. Finally, something seems to jog her memory. She gives me a soft smile that helps me relax a tiny bit.

That doesn't last long.

"Oh yes," she says. "You're the widow."

Until this point, I haven't thought about that term—or truly any label for my new relationship status. *Widow*—is that what I am? Is that the label for when your soul is dead and you're fighting to keep the other half alive? Before I can start truly chewing on that term, she redirects my attention with another question: "So what happened?"

---

* My goal is not to shame nor cause harm in the writing of this book. Therefore, I will leave this practitioner unnamed.

Again, I pause. I don't know how to begin answering this question. Do I start a long story of ten years of love or cut to the shorter story of a missed forty-five minutes that ends in death? I must have paused for too long. While my thoughts jumble about in my head, she redirects the question for me.

"Sometimes people find it helpful to start at the beginning of the day their partner died. Please feel free to start there. Or tell me about the moment you found out he was dead."

A small part of me is grateful for the additional instruction. A larger part of me is horrified. I've only told the full story of that night to the EMTs, the police, and the coroner. In fact, at this point I can barely remember anything that happened after I grabbed the phone to make the devastating 911 call . . . and I like it that way.

As the silence in the room lengthens, I can tell she is starting to feel uncomfortable. That is not helping my own internal uneasiness. And I haven't yet overcome my people-pleasing inclination that arises when somebody is uncomfortable. *Plus*, my brain whispers, *isn't discussing the pain what you're supposed to do in therapy? I mean, she's the grief specialist, and despite living immersed in it, I was no expert in grief. Maybe this is the process.*

I take a hasty sip from my water bottle and try again to identify my best next step: reviewing the entire day of the tragedy or simply sharing the end. I can feel my brain getting foggy, my head heavy as dissociation creeps in, a soothing steel blanket wrapping around me, shielding me from the pain.

With Therapist X still looking at me expectantly, I have a mental image of reaching into my skull and clawing apart that steel blanket so I can access my emotions. But the metal cocoon just keeps snapping back into place, cutting me off from the pain and blocking my ability to feel or even remember. Finally, in a robotic voice, I walk her through the final hours of John's life as I know them. Blunt data points pile up on the carpeted floor between us until, when I try to provide an ending to that awful night, my brain greets me with a yawning blackness of nothing. It seems I have no idea how I left that apartment and arrived at Michael and Ana's house. (To this day, I still don't.)

In response to my story, she quirks a single brow at me and delivers that famous therapist line: "And how did that make you feel?"

How did that make me feel?!?

She gets her answer this time. The steel blanket of numbness gives way to an avalanche of agony. A lifetime of loss and pain comes crashing down on me. I curl in on myself, a tiny ball on her sofa and my forehead drops onto my knees. A thought runs through my mind—*I just want to die*—but I have the presence of mind to know that I can't trust her with that statement. I simply shake my head, clutching my arms tightly around my knees, shuddering with each breath.

The minutes thunder severely in the silence as I attempt to ground myself back into my body. When I finally look up, I catch her staring at the clock.

"Unfortunately, Kate, that's all the time we have for today."

I am shocked, shaking; I can't gather my focus enough to say anything. A faint voice from the back of my mind volunteers the research I've studied that, in a moment of crisis, the prefrontal cortex (our "thinking brain") is less active (Shin et al., 2006), leaving us more emotionally activated and less able to think clearly. Meanwhile, Therapist X pulls out her paper calendar, clearly punctuating the end of our session.

"I have the same time available next week—does that work for you?"

When she looks up, it seems to finally register that I'm really not doing too well—curled up fetally on her sofa, breath shallow and ragged. She flips her calendar back a page.

"Perhaps sooner would be better? I can fit you in this Thursday afternoon at 2 p.m."

I nod woodenly, desperately grasping for my steel blanket of numbness; I can't quite pull it up over my head. The floor has dropped out from underneath me and I'm falling, falling.

"Yes, Thursday at 2 p.m."

I take the appointment card she hands me, gather my things, and exit the office into the bustling foyer. Only when I encounter the receptionist's look of alarm do I realize that I am weeping.

In the throes of trauma, the brain can protect us by disconnecting our ability to feel our bodies and our emotions (Zhang et al., 2016). Unfortunately, that does not mean it stops the looping thoughts, images, or sensations tied to trauma. Other systems in the brain allow those experiences of trauma to stay front and center (Repovs & Baddeley, 2006; Swick et al., 2017; Verwoerd et al., 2009; Shin et al., 2006).

Apparently, my brain and body have now convened a follow-up meeting and decided to dispense with my feel-good friend, dissociation. I sit in the baking heat of my car, my forehead resting on the steering wheel, feeling like I've allowed myself to be flayed open. Heartbreakingly, the level of amygdala activation—and thus fear reactivity—to revisiting traumatic stimuli is highly correlated to the onset of posttraumatic stress disorder (Leite et al., 2022). The events of that devastating night begin to play on loop in my brain, and with them, my own words echoing in my head: "I can't make him breathe."

CHAPTER 5

It's Not You—It's Your Brain

"I was taught that the human brain was the crowning glory of evolution so far, but I think it's a very poor scheme for survival."

—Kurt Vonnegut

For three days, my brain loops a Technicolor version of that awful night. Revisiting each step in agonizing clarity, dissecting my choices, taking me to some very dark places. Attempts to rest leave me reenacting that horrifying night; what little sleep I get is disrupted by nightmares.

When the brain is offered opportunity to rest, it may instead spiral us into *hypnagogic phenomena*—vivid visual experiences that are lived as a waking dream. When this phenomenon is driven by trauma, you can guess the content of these visuals. In traumatic experiences of loss, it has even been known for there to be a felt sense of the person who died (Horowitz, 2011; Lancel et al., 2021). This is the brain trying to make sense of the nonsensical.

On Thursday at 2 p.m., I walk back into that busy foyer and sit in the same chair. As if on cue, the receptionist throws me another look, more pointed this time.

"If you're here to see Dr. Blue, just go on up."

"No," I reply. "I have an appointment with Therapist X."

The receptionist shakes her head at me. "She's not here."

"Excuse me?"

"She already left for the day. She had a family situation to attend to. She said she had no appointments this afternoon."

A gnawing anxiety rises in my gut. "What do you mean she's gone?"

I had built up a story in my head that even though the first session had been terrible and the following three days even worse, this appointment would somehow bring me back to some semblance of balance. The world starts to feel floaty.

My voice climbs a couple octaves. "Please call her. We have an appointment."

"She said it's a family situation—I don't feel comfortable disrupting her. I'm sure you got the date and time wrong. Weren't you just here?"

Was this happening? Did I get the date and time wrong? No, she wrote it down. There's no way I had it wrong, right? I start to shake. Tears threaten to fall. *Oh gosh. This is awful. I'm losing control. What is wrong with me?!* In the back of my mind, I hear my thinking brain judging me, priming me for a shame spiral of epic proportions when I get back to the car. Right now, though, my survival brain is on the job.

I need this therapy session.

I'm scared.

I need help.

My voice, edged with panic, strangles out another piteous request. "Please call her."

I can tell the receptionist is getting nervous. Managing an adult woman on the verge of an emotional breakdown is probably not an everyday experience for her. Desperate, I fish around in my purse until the sharp point of the appointment card business card pricks my fingers. Triumphant, I brandish it at the receptionist. "See?"

Assessing the card, she begrudgingly picks up the phone. "Therapist X? I have a patient of yours here. She says you have an appointment. Her name is . . ." She looks at me inquiringly.

"Kate," I mouth at her.

"Uh, Kate. Is there something you would like for me to do?"

I hear Therapist X on the other end of the line. "Oh, shoot. I completely forgot about her. Let her know we can reschedule for next week. I need to go."

The receptionist hangs up and gives me a pitying look. "Would you like to reschedule?" she asks, still clearly annoyed but at least a little kinder.

I shake my head. *Absolutely not.* Internally, I'm still grappling for that steel blanket of dissociative numbness. It remains stubbornly absent. I don't know what I'm going to do.

I don't know what I'm going to do.

First, Do No Harm

So what happened that day in Therapist X's office? How did I transition from a state of numb but semi-functional grief to panic and despair? It started with two major missteps by the therapist before the session even began. First, she was extremely late, which meant leaving a highly anxious new patient in a chaotic public environment. Second, and most importantly, she failed to adequately review and prepare for our intake session—despite our earlier phone call and the direct referral from Dr. Blue, she did not even remember who I was. Running late is less than ideal, but we're all human, and I understand these things happen. However, both oversights created an environment that lacked psychological safety. Her in-session misstep, the worst one of all, was the failure to appropriately assess the safety of asking a trauma survivor to narrate the trauma experience. As a result of this grave mistake, I was retraumatized. Her absence at our follow-up appointment was the proverbial icing on the posttraumatic stress disorder cake. It fully shattered my protective barriers of dissociation, striking the raw nerves of abandonment and uncertainty.

Despite the negative impact on me, I don't blame Therapist X. In hindsight, I realize that she may have been a grief counselor, but she was most certainly not trained for what we today call *trauma-informed care*. In fact, it would not be until 2014 that the United States Department of Health and Human Services' Substance Abuse and Mental Health Services Administration (SAMHSA) released a formal paper defining trauma-informed care. Sitting with a patient who has experienced severe trauma requires specialized training to understand the impact of the therapeutic process on their highly vulnerable nervous system. In hindsight, I can feel grateful for this experience, awful as it was. It taught me that if I'm not able to show up fully resourced to care for my own patients, then I will not work as a doctor that day. As the Hippocratic oath reminds us, "first do no harm."

A Formal Introduction to Your Survival-Focused Friend "Amy"

Because the brain functions in such a unique and sometimes counterintuitive way, let's dig into what happens to a brain that has experienced trauma.

The pain, distress, and disturbances we humans experience and the "crazy" or irrational reactions, thoughts, and emotions that accompany them are driven by brain parts dedicated to our survival. These parts have been around far longer than our conscious Selves; however, they are not necessarily thoughtful or even logical. That's why, in moments of stress, survival will always win over logic.

Despite their incredible complexity, the brain has predictable working patterns, developed across millions of years of evolution. One of these patterns is to keep the things that help us survive and discard those that are no longer necessary or that impair us. Our brains, as well as our bodies, are designed to change, survive, and thrive across millennia and across the course of our unique lives. For example, some people today don't have wisdom teeth; science has highlighted that with time, they'll actually disappear from humans completely (Evans et al., 2016). In the same way, scientific studies show that the human brain has undergone significant changes throughout evolutionary history.

One such brain part is a pair of amygdalae that sit deep in the recesses of the brain. The amygdala is one of my absolute favorite brain regions due to its critical role in everything from keeping us alive to guiding purpose and passion in our lives (Cunningham & Brosch, 2012; Cunningham & Kirkland, 2013; Phelps et al., 2014). Scientists believe that these little almond-shaped structures showed up in the course of evolution approximately 300 million years ago (George & Blieck, 2011). But despite the fact that the amygdala has been supporting life for such a long time, the thinking brain often gets all the credit for our human experience.

In fact, the thinking brain, better known to science as the *prefrontal cortex*, is comparatively new to the evolutionary scene—making its presence known about 315,000 years ago (Tuttle, 2022). Some scientists claim that it took another 230,000 years for us to develop the capacity for language, social and cultural complexity, cognitive flexibility, and imagination, which is considered to be largely unique to humans (Powell et al., 2009; Harari, 2015). The prefrontal cortex is where our sense of Self and our thoughts and beliefs about the world are clarified and defined. It is also responsible for higher cognitive functions like reasoning, logical thought, and *metacognition*—that is, the ability to think about thinking. This ability is a very powerful thing; it is our key to self-reflection, the foundation for why psychotherapy works in the first place.

The fact that humans were able to survive for millions of years without a thinking brain highlights that survival doesn't actually require the ability to have a narrative story about one's experience or to share these stories. This can feel like surprising but normalizing data for many people who don't have memories of traumatic experiences but who still experience unexplained symptoms tied to trauma or painful life experiences. Instead, the amygdala speaks the language of the senses to ensure our survival. The human brain definitely follows a respect-your-elders ideology, especially when it comes to important matters such as life and death. And with the amygdala being a very old brain part—one of the great elders, if you will—this means it plays a significant role in defining our choices, thoughts, feelings, behaviors, and even relationships.

Several years ago, Dr. Louis Cozolino, a psychologist who pioneered integrating neuroscience into psychotherapy, coined the term *neurofluency* to describe a workable understanding of the neuroscience underlying what our brains cause us to do as we navigate the world. Neurofluency creates a whole new approach for understanding our very human reactions and responses to the world, especially those driven by our primal friend the amygdala . . . or, as I like to call it, *Amy*. By personifying the amygdala, we can more easily separate out what the primal, survival-oriented brain is doing from what our logical, grounded Self would choose to do. I experienced this firsthand with Amy, as she drove my behavior with intrusive memories and flashbacks while my Self brain struggled to catch up with science and reason.

This separation is extremely important because, as mentioned earlier, Amy doesn't prioritize our quality of life. Not because she is harmful, but because she is a fierce and protective warrior who is always doing her best to have our backs and will use whatever resources are at her disposal. She doesn't see the world through the lens of logical and socially approved human engagement. Instead, Amy experiences the world through the lens of our senses and our most primitive survival-based feelings. As a result, she will often drive us to do illogical things in the name of protecting us from danger and ensuring our survival. Sometimes this means encouraging behaviors like drinking too much, overeating, road rage, or self-injury. Your thinking brain knows these behaviors are less than preferable, but Amy knows they will quickly help numb or soothe the pain and distress you're experiencing. Amy prioritizes short-term relief because in a moment of survival, the next second is far more important than tomorrow, let alone next month or next year.

When you find yourself struggling to choose the logical, grounded thing to do and you're not getting there, I encourage you to remember that it's not you—it's your brain. Understanding Amy is important because it gives you the opportunity to view yourself more compassionately in those more "crazy" or "out of control" human moments.

So how does Amy take care of you? You may recall those three core principles of survival related to Self that I introduced in chapter 3: *Am I safe? Am I lovable and do I belong? Am I successful?* I refer to these as *Amy's Core Values* because they are her driving force for helping you navigate the world. As you move through your surroundings, you are picking up sensory information around you, and all that you see, smell, hear, taste, and touch is being processed in your brain at a rate four times faster than the blink of an eye, just 75 milliseconds. In that time, the amygdala filters all that data to determine whether it needs to be acted upon (Méndez-Bértolo et al., 2016). Like any good threat assessor, Amy also compares the present data with your past experiences and what you have seen or heard about from others, much like a mental Google search. If anything seems possibly concerning to Amy, she will pop up a warning flag that says, "Hey! This data reminds me of that other scary/uncomfortable/stressful thing that happened before."

The information coming into your brain eventually reaches your prefrontal cortex as well, but it takes approximately 350 milliseconds (about the blink of an eye) to get there. In other words, when you react from a space of fear or rage, your thinking brain often has not even yet kicked in. In some situations, your thinking brain may not be consulted at all. If Amy senses a big enough threat, real or perceived, she can actually shut down your prefrontal cortex to divert power to your more primal survival systems (Shin et al., 2006). The more power Amy is pulling to run her Google searches, the less power is available to the thinking brain.

Let's revisit: Blink once. With a speed four times (*four times!*) faster than a blink, Amy is doing a threat assessment. If an appropriate level of threat, real or perceived, is noted, she has the opportunity to take over the brain in her best attempt to keep us safe.

Now that we've established this understanding of how Amy works within the brain as a whole, let's return to my appointment with Therapist X.

Since John's death, my brain had created a very effective buffer of numbing dissociation between the events of that night and the rest of my world. Even while I was navigating a deep sense of loss and grief with my prefrontal cortex, Amy had been utilizing the highly successful survival strategy of numbing to hold back the waves of darkness. When Therapist X asked me to walk her through the details of that night, she was essentially inviting Amy to unleash the torrent of trauma-driven data of John's death with no dissociation to keep me cushioned from it. As a result, I reexperienced that night in vivid and excruciating clarity. The darkness of my grief and loss combined with the reliving of the narrative rapidly overtook my brain, swallowing me in the full gut-wrenching experience of all the sensory and emotional data Amy had gathered on the night of his death.

In that first appointment, Therapist X was (I believe accidentally) engaging in an *exposure intervention*, a common part of traditional trauma treatment dating back to the birth of prolonged exposure in the mid-1980s (Foa & Kozak, 1986). A vital element of this work is that after weeks of gradual interventions and appropriate preparation, the patient is eventually guided to reimmerse themselves in the moment of the traumatic encoding. The problem is that when we're narrating a trauma story, whatever distance we might have created between our sense of Self and the narrative is now eliminated; there is no protection to keep the brain from being retraumatized. This problem is widely recognized today and has paved the way for newer trauma therapies—such as eye movement desensitization and reprocessing (EMDR), Havening Techniques®, tapping, somatic experiencing, and others—to become standard practice for processing trauma.

I have no reason to believe that Therapist X was consciously attempting to do prolonged exposure with me. I believe she was distracted by personal issues* and uninformed in how to properly address trauma. The cost of her mistake was clumsy therapy with disastrous and dangerous consequences. Furthermore, her no-show at our following session recreated all the other times in my life when I desperately needed someone to be there for me but was left alone in pain.

Cozolino (2016, p. 6) highlights that "90% of the input to the cortex comes from internal neural processing, not the outside world." This means that 90 percent of each present moment is defined by experiences from our past. Let that sink in for a moment: *Only 10 percent of what your brain is noticing right now is actually from the present.* The other 90 percent of how you are experiencing this moment, what you are feeling and what you are thinking, comes from your brain filling in the blanks with information from your past. For Amy, and ultimately for us, this means the past is always present. We not only need to show compassion for ourselves on the way to healing, but we also need to show Amy a little love and understanding.

Given that I had been researching and working with individuals with trauma for ten years at that point, you might think I would be immune from getting stuck in the mental agony of PTSD. But as we've discussed, when it comes to trauma, thinking does not win. All my knowledge and training couldn't keep me from getting mired in the darkness.

---

* I learned later that Therapist X had experienced a death of a family member that same week and that she missed the Thursday appointment to attend the funeral.

This is what brains can do to humans in the name of survival.

However, given the chance, the darkness also holds opportunities for incredible growth.

CHAPTER 6

Phoenix

"We are like islands in the sea, separate on the surface but connected in the deep."

—William James

Have you ever walked through your home at night, no lights on, yet easily navigated across the room without making a sound or stumbling into the furniture?

Or raided the refrigerator at 3 a.m. and instantly located the leftover pizza or ice cream, despite still being half-asleep?

Have you ever wondered how you can accomplish such extraordinary feats?

Deep in the recesses of the brain, in the entorhinal cortex* to be exact, we have tiny cells called *object-trace cells* (Qasim et al., 2019; Tsao et al., 2013) that interpret the distance and direction of things in our environment relative to where we are. In the same brain area, there are *place cells,* which mark our experiences in specific locations, like dropping pins on a phone's map app (O'Keefe, 1976; O'Keefe, 2014). Place cells are what call up an image of our

---

* The brain's entorhinal cortex is considered a network hub or gateway for temporal perception, navigation, and memory.

partners walking in from work when we hear the garage door open or of our friends when someone asks us what they're up to these days.

In chapter 3, we discussed how our brains build frameworks to help us make sense of the world. Object-trace cells and place cells play a critical role in this endeavor. They let us know where things are, whether they are in the room with us (object-trace cell) or where they are expected to be (place cell). This makes it so we don't have to recreate the world every time we want to interact (or not) with something in our familiar environment.

Of course, sometimes our familiar environment changes. Rearrange the room by day, and we may end up with some bruised shins in the dead of night until the new arrangement becomes familiar. In the same way, these little cells carry on lighting up around the expected locations of our loved ones even when the conscious brain knows they're no longer with us (O'Connor, 2022). Just as it takes a long time for a cartographer to draw a map of somewhere previously uncharted, it takes a long time for our brains to build these connections or to rebuild them when someone leaves us. We are left with a brain still firing with expectation for them to be where they've always been, which then becomes a brain grappling with devastating fear and confusion once that expectation fades and we can no longer envision where they are. As neuroscientist and grief expert Mary-Frances O'Connor (2022) eloquently reminds us, "The idea that a person simply does not exist anymore does not follow the rules the brain has learned over a lifetime."

No One Likes Death

I wake with a start and roll over, feeling his presence in the bed beside me. Anticipating his warmth, his sleepy smile, I reach out.

Nothing. It's cold, empty. My brain quickly recalculates. *He's a night owl, he's probably in the living room working.* I swing my legs and get out of bed, easily navigating the bedroom furniture, and emerge into the great room. Empty. No light from a laptop. No soft tunes coming through his headphones. Nothing.

Too quickly, the fog of sleep clears from my head. *Kate. He's dead. When are you going to get it through your head? He'll never be here again.*

My heart hurts—a visceral ache of loss and agony. His presence felt so real just a minute ago. I sigh wearily and glance at the kitchen clock. 4 a.m. The idea of returning to the bedroom and trying to sleep for another hour or two fills me with dread. Resigned, I head to the kitchen and start the coffee maker. It's going to be another long day.

Different versions of this waking nightmare had been periodically plaguing me since the night John died, and they have become an almost nightly occurrence after the disastrous experience in Therapist X's office. When my brain isn't reliving the moment I found him and couldn't make him breathe, it teases me with the possibilities of traveling back in time, setting me up to wake and then realize he's gone all over again.

But this time felt different. Perhaps it's the exhaustion of reliving his death every night. Perhaps it's the cycling symptoms of PTSD and their grinding toll on my mind and body. This time, however, he'd been tangible. It felt like he was really there. I fear I am truly losing my mind.

The next day, I tell my mom about it—the bizarre searching in my soul, the continual ache of rediscovery, the fear that I was going crazy. With all the love in the world, she gives me a hug and gently says, "I know, honey. It hurts. He's gone. You really need to start looking forward."

Her arms offer the comfort that her words lack. I know she's doing her best to help, and I can't disagree with her. As unwilling as I am to let go of John, looking forward seems more and more like a relief compared to reliving this heartbreak day after day. But how to begin? No one seems to have the answer to that question.

Modern humans are really bad at death. When mortality comes knocking, we are forced to grapple with it amid a glut of billion-dollar industries hyping the necessity of being forever young, healthy, and vibrant. Those immersed in grief, half-yearning to join the deceased, often find their living loved ones have scattered to the winds—real-life ghosting. This phenomenon is so common that grief researcher Dr. Alan Wolfelt has created a philosophy around how relationships change following death, one that follows my own experience to a scary tee. He posits that people orbiting a grieving person can be broken down into three groups: neutral, harmful, and empathetic (Wolfelt, 2016).

In the wake of death and tragic loss, a third of your people will stay in your orbit but be *neutral*. They don't hinder you in your healing journey, but they don't really help you either. These are the people who will check in with a casual "how are you" should you cross paths on the street or at work. For the survivor, the relationship may feel intuitively but indescribably different. These people are present but distant. The real-world living of the elephant in the room that no one dares to discuss.

The *harmful* third are those people who become toxic or absent altogether. These people are detrimental to your personal efforts to heal, though not necessarily on purpose. Remember, we are dealing with the power of mortality here. Watching you try to manage your life in the midst of grief may activate their amygdala similarly to your own. Some people will just go *poof!* out of your life; often, it can sadly be the last people you would expect to disappear. That's what happened with much of Johnny's family and also with some people who I thought were my dearest friends, my chosen family. Death brings more losses than just the loss of the one who is no longer walking alongside us in this temporal world.

Navigating the complexities of the harmful third involves establishing healthy boundaries. It's undeniably tough to navigate grief and simultaneously communicate that you can't keep certain people in your life, whether temporarily or permanently. Nevertheless, these boundaries are crucial for your healing journey. Taking care of your emotional well-being means recognizing how others' actions and reactions affect you and safeguarding your space for processing and healing.

The last third—I like to think of these people as the "therapeutic third"—will prove to be *empathetic*. They are the ones who show up with a warm pot of chili at dinnertime and leave it on the doorstep, waving and blowing a kiss as they head to their car, right about the time you were wondering and fretting over how you were going to pull it together long enough to make something for dinner. These people hold you up on the days when you find yourself barely able to breathe. As I mentioned, I had a group of women who rotated shifts sleeping at my house for a while—every night a different friend hanging out in my bedroom, making sure I was okay, just being there while I battled my internal demons of grief, trauma, and loss. Sometimes subtle, sometimes incredible, the acts of love from this empathetic third are a powerful force of healing.

Still, being ghosted by some of our nearest and dearest will alter our sense of safety and connection in the world. Letting people into the mysterious effects of those object trace- and place-cell moments can seem unwise, even downright dangerous, lest we risk losing another person. In this way, grief has many sociological parallels to trauma. As both a grief and trauma specialist, I have repeatedly heard my patients share a fear that they are crazy because of the things their brain is manifesting. The fear is what makes us feel unable to connect with our community or even another person. The alienation we feel causes us to spiral even lower, the hijacked amygdala driving us deeper into a sense of being lost and hopeless, perhaps even sprinkling in some shame, the amygdala's "secret sauce" for ensuring these survival lessons stick.

Although I had empathetic people around me, I felt deeply isolated and alone in my experience. The only time I felt safe telling my story of loss and grief was when I scribbled in my old journal or raged at the universe in the dark vortex of my thoughts. There was nobody who could truly understand or even hold space for my grief during those awfullest of times.

That was about to change.

From Death Comes a Breath of Life

Shortly after John's death, I begin my doctoral internship with the County of San Bernardino at the Phoenix Community Counseling Center. With my brain still deeply immersed in the black depths of sorrow, it's all I can do to stay present and aware in the fast-paced world of county mental health. Nevertheless, I throw myself into the work, relieved to have a list of action items to structure my day, to reconnect with my sense of purpose, and to work with my incredible supervisor Dr. Dianne Wolkenhauer and the Phoenix team I will grow to love over the next year.

From my first day at the clinic, a strange question begins to follow me: "Have you met Lena?"

The question comes from so many different individuals that it quickly becomes unsettling. When I ask why they are asking, I'm met with the same cryptic answer: "She needs to tell you herself."

I gather that most of the clinic staff has been told some version of my story; this provides a sense of safety and space for me to begin work without having to explain why I'm starting work several weeks after the rest of my internship cohort. However, the contrast between the team's full knowledge of my recent loss and their cryptic references to this person I'm supposed to meet, coupled with Lena's prolonged absence from the clinic, do little to soothe the growing unease in my gut.

A few weeks into my tenure at Phoenix, my eyes meet Lena's. I know it's her because her gaze shines with the same haunted light that follows my every waking step. One of my supervisors, Dr. Boyer, a presence of warmth and wisdom, approaches.

"Kate, have you met Lena? Lena, have you met Kate?"

We both shake our heads, eyeing each other cautiously. Lena is the first to speak.

"I've been hearing about you," she says. "People have told me that you're here."

Anxiety begins knocking on my brain. *Oh god, what horrible story do we share?* That familiar pit in my stomach begins making its presence known. *Do I want to know?*

"Do you have a moment to talk?" I ask quietly. She nods, seeming similarly apprehensive.

The path from the clerical bay to my tiny office is short, but the journey there feels long and leaden. Once there, we sit and simply stare at each other for a couple of endless minutes. Though I know nothing of her, I feel a depth of sorrow, gravity, and grief in this woman's face that belies her youthful countenance, that reflects my own shattered world. Something inside me shifts and crumbles open; suddenly, I know that I'm no longer alone.

Eventually one of us—I don't know who—gently breaks the all-encompassing silence and queries, "What happened?"

Our stories are different but deeply similar. Within a week of John's death, Lena's fiancé hadn't come home. Rather than the sound of his key in the door, her anxious worry had been met by the knock of a police officer, there to tell her that her fiancé had been in a car accident that resulted in his death. In that moment, her world blew into a million pieces just like mine had.

As she tells me the story, my mental movie reel unfolds: a young woman anxiously calling her fiancé, his lack of response a conspicuous rarity. The bile starts to rise in my throat as I remember my own frantic calls to John, my bewildered anxiety, other people's placating response: "It's fine."

The bile turns to bitterness as the story continues. A knock at the door for her, the apartment lights on and a locked front door for me. Her slowly opening the door to the sight of a police officer, her gasp of *No!* before he says a word, her dawning horror at what his presence means. Me circling the bed and finding the lamp knocked over, John collapsed beside it. Both our narratives already played out to their final conclusion even before we are told, "It's too late." And then, the searing agony of the unavoidable truth. Souls reduced to whispers. Plans torn asunder. The once warm bed forever cold. The question of *Why?* now the only certainty.

It's unfathomable to me: Here, at the Phoenix Clinic, is another human living out this surreal voyage of grief and devastation. How could it be that in a population of 307 million people, she and I were sitting across from each other in this moment? I didn't know how to make sense of it. According to the National Center for Health Statistics (2009, as cited in Kochanek et al., 2011), only

118,021 people of all ages died in the United States as a result of an accident. That's a 0.0004% chance of this woman and I meeting within one year, let alone beginning our journeys into widowhood within weeks of one another.

I had applied to twenty internship locations throughout California, but Phoenix had always been my top choice. Not only did I dearly want to work alongside Dr. Wolkenhauer, but working there would also allow me to continue overseeing my research at the university while staying within an hour's drive of my family, John's family, and many of my dearest friends. I could have been matched with many different clinics, but the one placement I wanted was the one where I was placed. Now, nine days into my internship, I knew exactly why I was there.

In that moment, sitting with Lena, I experience understanding and relief, two sensations that had been completely lost to me since the night of June 13. Lena and I give each other permission to be in the darkness of loss and grief and death. In doing so, we are finally able to normalize it.

We're not crazy.

We're not alone.

Grief Changes Not Only You, But Also Your Relationship to Others

In the throes of grief, the relationship between the mind and body experience vacillates drastically. On some days, the mind seems to show up for work but the body drags along behind, each moment pulling you deeper into despair. On other days, the body will bound out of bed, ready to conquer the world, while the brain remains immersed in a fog—or worse, drowning in the bittersweet memories of the past.

Since my unfortunate appointment with Therapist X, I could not seem to get my brain to stop swirling. My amygdala was running the show and I had absolutely no gauge for what was normal grief and what was pathological. But having a fellow traveler on this journey began to buffer the crippling suspicion that I was losing my mind.

In the weeks that follow, Lena and I take full advantage of the extraordinary opportunity to share our grief and pain with another person who really understands. Some nights we spend binge watching reality TV and eating junk food, wanting to feel like normal human beings again. On other nights, we unpack our stories and our symptoms, trying to piece back together who we were. We examine how our grief and loss have impacted our sense of Self and the effects they are having on our minds and bodies. We attempt to express the *why* behind the emotions we are experiencing—the anger, disappointment, helplessness, abandonment. It helps us acknowledge our losses and have self-compassion for what we are feeling.

Lena and I share all of this without shame or embarrassment. To be able to be completely lost, insanely broken, laughably devastated, enraged, and profoundly confused alongside another human begins to build a new form of balance and trust for me.

As Oprah Winfrey has famously said, "Life always whispers to you first, but if you ignore the whisper, sooner or later you'll get a scream." Our brains and bodies don't like it when we're not paying attention to the whispers. The more we ignore the data they're putting in front of us, the louder and more intrusive it will become. In times of mourning, much like surviving trauma, we become skilled at tucking away our pain, fearing rejection or further loss. Yet we desperately need a village, just like young children do, to help us heal. In the aftermath of heavy experiences, our core survival values—*Am I safe? Am I lovable and do I belong? Am I successful?*—are nurtured and reinforced by the new "villages" we intentionally create. The village Lena and I started together allowed us to rediscover and reconnect with the empathetic ones in our communities who were willing and eager to stick with us.

The universe bringing Lena into my world became one of the greatest gifts in my life. We take to calling each other "Wifey" in honor of what we were supposed to be before fate had taken that opportunity from us. It feels to me like the universe had ensured we would not be alone. And from our deepest depths of sorrow, Lena and I hold each other throughout our recovery journeys.

CHAPTER 7

Fallen Angel

"Owning our story can be hard but not nearly as difficult as spending our lives running from it. Embracing our vulnerabilities is risky but not nearly as dangerous as giving up on love and belonging and joy—the experiences that make us the most vulnerable. Only when we are brave enough to explore the darkness will we discover the infinite power of our light."

—Brené Brown

By this point, I am sure you are wondering about the story behind what happened to John. I'll be blunt: This is one of the most painful parts of this story to share. There are still times when I find I can speak more readily about the throes of my trauma than I can about what led to John's death.

Let's face it head-on; it's time to rip the bandaid off.

Desperate to understand what led to my beloved fiancé, a man in his early thirties who suddenly died one week before his wedding, I spend the two months after his death communicating with Betsy at the Los Angeles County Coroner's Office. She is so sweet and kind, seeming to sense the depths of my despair and going above and beyond to help me understand what had happened. If

Betsy ever reads this book, I hope she understands how vital her warmth and kindness were to the desperate young woman I was at that time.

At 3:04 p.m. on August 5, 2009, the following email arrives in my inbox from the Los Angeles County Coroner's Office:

To: *****@yahoo.com

From: *******@coroner.lacounty.gov

Subject: Case Number ####-#######

Hello Kate,

John's cause of death was finalized today as Multiple Drug Intoxication with the manner of death as Accident. He had several drugs in his system above the therapeutic range including Tramadol, Oxycodone, Soma, and Valium. For a complete list including levels of the medications present please contact the Records Section at (xxx)xxx-xxxx to obtain a copy of the toxicology report.

Please call me if there is anything else I can help you with.

Betsy

My world falls out from underneath me. What feels like ice-cold water fills my veins, chilling me to my core.

Multiple drug intoxication?!

My deepest fear had come to life.

The Story of the Spiral

The story of John's death began two years earlier, when his body began to decay under the weight of a mysterious sickness. He never felt well; his body was in constant pain. There was scabbing around his eyes, on his eyelids and mouth, and he had a general rash all over his body. Any areas where skin folded or creased held open sores. His body burned and ached so much that anything more than basic touch was out of the question; needless to say, our physical intimacy was nonexistent. The closest thing we had was me applying prescription creams to his body to ease the pain, soothe the open wounds, and reduce the itching of the scabs.

His opioid and benzodiazepine use was medically sanctioned, greenlit by more prescription pads than I care to admit. While obtaining a bottle of pills was suddenly as easy as getting a candy bar at the drugstore, what we couldn't get was a clear diagnosis nor a treatment plan. Instead, I had spent nearly two years watching the vibrant man I loved transform into a weak, self-conscious, and deeply pained human who could not move about in his daily life without agony. Despite the sixty hours a week I split between attending graduate school classes, working at the VA, managing the Loma Linda University Psychology Department training clinic, and completing my dissertation, I commuted to his house, an hour away in Playa del Rey, several times a week to provide caretaker support.*

Sleep was a rarity for us both. My excuse was being in the final stages of my doctorate program; John's was a form of a circadian rhythm disorder** that he had struggled with throughout his life. Despite knowing that his erratic sleep patterns only worsened his stress and his excruciating pain, he rarely gave himself permission

---

* At that time, John lived in Los Angeles while I was still completing my graduate studies and living an hour away in Loma Linda.

** Circadian rhythm sleep disorders are caused by desynchronization between internal sleep-wake rhythms and the light-darkness cycle. Patients typically have insomnia, excessive daytime sleepiness, or both, which typically resolve as the body clock realigns itself.

to rest. An average weekend saw me begging John to put his laptop away, silence his phone, and prioritize his health, only to have him tease me that I was the pot calling the kettle black. John's drive to be in service of others was one of his amygdala's core values. He also had a deeply rooted sense of family loyalty that was inherent to his sense of Self. These two experiences were intensely woven together in his work managing the information technology side of the family business while also building a small business with a good friend.

Even as I fought to exhaustion to get him the help he needed, I was becoming increasingly concerned that he was abusing the pain medication his doctors were giving him. We had many conversations about my concerns; he blew them off at first, but became increasingly defensive as the months went by.

One afternoon, about six months before he died, I went to grab something from the refrigerator in our garage and found an unexpectedly open box of old medications. It had been years since I had used the Percocet and Vicodin in the box; they'd been prescribed for a serious back injury in my early twenties. The scientist in me saw an opportunity to test my hypothesis—since confronting him had yielded no information, why not simply gather data? Guided half by fear and half by scientific rigor, I pulled out the bottles and counted the pills before returning them to the box.

I loved this man with my entire being and truly believed we would find our way back to the intimate, trusting relationship we once had. My job during this time, though, was to be for him what he had been for me when we first met—the safe landing, the regulator, the caretaker, the support, and the unconditional love. What I ultimately missed is that this would create the perfect setup for me to be his enabler.

A Little Bit of Magic

By 2009, John's worsening condition made it harder and harder for him to engage with the outside world. Often, it took considerable pushing to get him to venture outside once he crash-landed at my home. The bribe of "Let's go to Starbucks" always held some weight, which could then be followed by whatever errands we had to run. On this particular evening, the task was getting food for our dog, Roscoe.

***

John's car clock marks our arrival at PetSmart at 8:57 p.m., just three minutes before it closes. I rush in, anticipating the harried looks of the remaining clerks. Instead, though, I find a small group of people gathered in a huddle—store clerks as well as some people from the PetSmart Adoption Program, which I'd volunteered with in the past. As I approach, one of them catches sight of me and waves me over, then bends down and scoops up a wiggling little body. My heart begins to sink. I know where this is going. They need a foster home. I silently curse John for his poor timing—why on earth was I at PetSmart at 9 p.m. anyway?!

And then a tiny puppy, only six weeks old, is dumped into my cupped hands. It curls up into my palms and raises its eyes, blinking at me. I have no opportunity to resist.

The program volunteers tell me that the puppy's litter had been left in a taped-up box on the train tracks. Little puppies, so little they could almost sit in your hand. They had been left, I suppose, with the presumption that they would be killed by the next speeding train. An incredibly heartbreaking start to life for these young pups. By pure luck, a human savior heard them yipping and whining in the box and brought them to the store that morning. The volunteers tell me they are staying open late because this one, the runt of the litter, still hasn't been fostered. They don't want to have to take her to the shelter in town—she is so little.

It is impossible to say no to those big brown eyes, that intoxicating puppy smell. I am a goner.

I rescued Roscoe at a mere eight weeks old, but that was five years ago. I have no provisions—and even less time—for a tiny dog. But the next thing I know, I'm cradling the pup while the PetSmart employees and adoption staff gather around, piling up supplies, detailing instructions. Without my noticing, almost 45 minutes have passed. I am immersed in conversation with the adoption group when the automatic doors sweep open and I hear the unmistakable sound of John's flip-flops. I try to arrange the puppy in the cutest position possible, then slowly turn to greet him, a huge smile plastered on my face. My plan is to lead with the opportunity to help—this man has the biggest heart of anyone I have ever met— then reel him in with the puppy smell.

"Johnny . . . she needs a foster home."

Much like what had been done to me, I push the little pup into his arms and nestle her right under his nose.

His eyes flash with humor. He knows exactly what I'm doing. Even through the haze of his sickness and pain, he has an uncanny ability to read me. He pulls the puppy away and holds her in front of him, assessing her, me, and the situation. The people around me freeze, sensing that the moment of decision is at hand. He sighs audibly, then rests the puppy on his upturned forearm, cradling her tiny head in his hand. Staring me down, he states in an unusually authoritative voice, "Fostering only."

Everyone relaxes, except for me. I am taken aback by his reaction. John is a huge animal lover. Back in the early 2000s, when I was going through my EMDR training, I had asked him where his ideal safe place would be. Without hesitation, he replied, "A room full of puppies!"

He had also been talking for years about wanting another dog. The moment passes but lingers in my mind, enough that I ask to drive on the way home so John will hold the little pup and get better acquainted.

Over the weekend, I fall head over heels in love with her, while John becomes increasingly agitated and nervous. He keeps circling back to our litany of responsibilities: the upcoming wedding, his job, my dissertation, my internship. He adamantly repeats, "We do not have the time and energy for this."

He's right, of course. What's startling is that he has rarely been the bastion of logic in our relationship. John is the idealist, the optimist, the we-can-do-it-all conqueror. But over the past two years, as his strength continued to wane and his pain grew, he'd become increasingly pragmatic, borderline pessimistic. Unbeknownst to me, the sense that he was going to die soon was already brewing in his mind and body.

When Monday rolled around, his resolve remains steadfast. "We're taking her back," he says. "We do not have the ability to take this on right now. I'm sick, we don't know what's going on, and we're getting married soon."

I look at him with tears in my eyes but don't argue. Instead, I walk back into the bedroom to where the pup sits on our bed, chewing on her tiny giraffe-shaped rope toy. When I walk in, she half bounds, half stumbles over herself to greet me. Despite myself, I start to weep.

The Devastating Reality

For the record, this is all insanely unlike me. During this time in my life, I've returned to some of my past coping skills, becoming deeply emotionally compartmentalized as I stretch beyond my limits as John's caretaker and the experience of watching my person physically disintegrate in front me with no clear rhyme or reason. My tears are not actually about the puppy; they're about the brief moments of joy we've experienced, watching Roscoe and her play during the previous two days. Hearing John's laughter, seeing him finally put aside his work to pay attention to something that makes his heart happy. Maybe he feels it too. Hearing my emotion, he follows me into the room with a gentle "Hey . . ." and wraps his arms around me. Despite his body's instinctive tensing as his shirt grabs at his raw skin and the pressure of contact ignites his inflamed muscles, he holds on to me when I try to pull away.

"It's okay, Kitten," he says. "We'll keep her."

At this, I cry even harder.

"Shhh," he whispers. "We're keeping her."

In honor of his favorite childhood story, *Peter Pan*, John names the puppy Tinkerbell after the magical pixie who kept ever-present watch over the boy who never grew up. The Tinkerbell in the story was always loyal to those she loved, and her four-legged namesake uniquely brought out that same quality in her new two-legged father. I have no idea how important this little runt will be in the coming months and years. She will prove to be a constant living link to brighter times, a foothold of meaning when the landscape of my traumatized brain desperately needs it.

Hard Conversations, Deception, and Enablement

The time inevitably comes to get Tinkerbell spayed, and it just happens to align with my last university exams week. When I say last, I mean last *ever*—the final quarter of my doctoral program. I have a straight-A average, but I'm wobbling under the pressure of trying to protect it. Perhaps because of the stress I'm feeling, we start having harder and harder conversations about John's increasing use of opioids and benzodiazepines. I begin to speak plainly about my fears that this is no longer about pain management but instead is becoming dependency. I tell him that I understand he's intentionally numbing his brain and body so he can continue to work, to be his best Self for his family and for me. But, I add, I'm scared that he is hurting himself.

I can tell he is scared too. His drive to be the best for everyone else is impairing his ability to take care of himself. His intentions and purpose are honorable though, which makes it all the harder for him to admit his problem. Arguing with someone whose identity is deeply entwined in self-sacrifice is exhausting, especially when the focus of the argument is removing substances that are necessary for the self-sacrifice to continue. Pushing himself to exhaustion maintained his Self story: *I have value because I care, I tend, I take care of . . .* Those survival core values from childhood run deep.

The weekend before Tinkerbell's appointment, I catch him in a lie that he cannot deny. Remember the open box in the garage refrigerator? Within several weeks, more than half of the pills are gone. Armed with data to confirm my fears, I confront him about the disappearing medication.

He attempts to insinuate other people are stealing it—a horrifying lie that shoves me out of my loving, supportive mindset and forces me to take an extreme view of the situation. *He is not a liar . . . but here he is, lying. He is a protector, yet he's making an accusation that, if I believed it, would have had very serious consequences for people in our lives, people that we love and trust.* This, I recognize, is addiction behavior.

Our discussions escalate to full-blown fights, harrowing and heartbreaking fights that neither of us has the strength for. The data is undeniable, but so is his stubbornness.

Working with a patient in the throes of addiction is fundamentally different from being in an intimate relationship with someone paralyzed by addiction. My boundaries are blurred; the science matters a lot less and the heart matters a lot more. Eventually, I cave. Since I cannot force him into treatment and I want to respect his privacy—he was adamant his family could not know—we make a plan: I will keep his prescribed medications in a hidden lockbox and dispense them in the quantities noted by his doctor. We agree that if he takes more painkillers on any given day than he was prescribed, then he will forfeit those medications for the rest of the week. He was always so proud of his self-control. Here was his opportunity to show me.

To show me. Even as I write this, nausea rises inside me at the hubris of believing I could manage this alone. But at that time, my weary mind rationalizes that it's just one more step toward helping him heal. Driven by love and fear, I become the manager of his addiction—a tale as old as time of enabling and secrecy. A story doomed to end in failure.

I was a fool.

A blind, loving fool.

The Whispers of What Was to Come

The day of Tinkerbell's spaying surgery starts just like any other day. I wrestle with John to get him out of bed, ply him with promises of amazing coffee, and eventually load man and dog into the car. Watching them turn the corner, I release a long, exhausted sigh. Two more days of finals are all that lie between me and the breathing room I need to take care of this man who carries my heart, who desperately needs me to help him make different choices. I am committed to giving him what he gave me in the darkest hours of my early twenties: support, insight, a chance to heal.

John drops Tinkerbell off for her routine procedure with our veterinarian, returns home to work for a few hours, then heads back to the vet's office to pick her up. Everything goes fine, until the moment it doesn't. That moment begins on Barton Road, just four blocks from the veterinarian's office, when Tinkerbell starts bleeding. Not stitches-popping-open bleeding, but profuse, car-covered-in-blood bleeding.

I see it unfold in my mind's eye: Panicking, John executes a crazy U-turn on the narrow, winding road just before the Loma Linda University Medical Center and careens back to the vet. Heart racing, adrenaline flooding, he gently eases out of the car, puppy in hand, and bounds into the office. "Help! She's dying!" He's told that they don't have the equipment needed to save her, that he must take her to the urgent care facility, one town over.

Stunned, John quickly bolts back to the car, tiny Tinkerbell in his arms. He's driving wildly as his mind plays through the awful moment when he has to tell me that our sweet puppy died. In ten years together, his mantra was he would never let me down. He will not fail me. She will not die. He guns the engine faster.

John spends the next eight hours at the veterinary urgent care, staying in touch with me, telling me what's going on with Tinkerbell alongside stories about the veterinary staff and the fellow pet parent with whom he'd shared a Camel Light in the parking lot. He won't leave—in his mind, his presence ensures Tinkerbell's survival.

"Do you need me to come over? What can I do for you?" I keep asking.

In true John fashion, he assures me, "No Kitten, I've got this. You have two more exams tomorrow, and you need a good night's sleep. I've got this. I've made friends with the veterinary staff; I brought everybody coffee. I'll be home when I can."

This is so John: making friends everywhere he goes, taking care of everyone, never letting on how stressed or worried he is. I knew he was taught to never prioritize his emotions; others' emotions were the ones that mattered. Give, care for, and then give and care for some more—that's our Johnny. It's his nature, his core identity, and ultimately his demise.

Knowing he wanted me to study, I hunker down and focus on my studies. In a way, I am soothed because he is up and out of the house with no medication on him. *I've locked it up, he doesn't know where it is, and I have the key.*

It's around eleven or twelve that night when he finally comes home with Tinkerbell, frazzled and exhausted. I make him some food and put him into bed. But he can't go to sleep before asking me, "When is your first exam? You have to wake me up so I can keep an eye on her. Can you stay up and watch her right now?"

"Of course, honey. I'll just study. I'll sit next to her. She's sleeping. We're going to be okay."

I didn't know it then, but we would never be okay.

At 8:45 a.m., I wake him up, make him some breakfast.

"Watch some TV, relax," I tell him. "Don't get on your laptop. Please don't work. Just rest; you're exhausted. This has been emotionally taxing. Working will make your pain worse. Call in sick. Please give yourself some time."

I see his gaze sliding over to his phone, already flooded with text messages and missed calls. I contemplate taking it with me, maybe even his laptop too. But I don't want to face the wrath of his family, were I to cut them off from their technology guru. Instead, I tuck the computer and phone away in my office and settle John on the sofa with Tinkerbell resting beside him. A quick kiss to his forehead and I'm off.

I take my exams, wrap up some final preparation for my internship, and pick up our favorite bean and cheese burritos on my way home. I'm glad to find his car hasn't moved since I left. I am hopeful I will find him asleep.

I am not at all prepared for what I see instead: John, on the sofa, head rolled back, a blank stare fixated on the ceiling.

My heart jumps into my throat.

"John!"

Both he and Tinkerbell lift their heads and stare at me, startled. *What on earth?* is all I can think. He looked for all the world like the newly dead bodies I had seen working in hospice, vacant eyes and gaping mouths.

"Hey, Kitten." His words slur together as his head returns to rest and his hand moves to gently stroke Tinkerbell. "How'd it go?"

Something is deeply off. I practically tiptoe into the room, assessing the situation, no sudden moves lest a detail be hidden or covered up. I gently place the burritos down on the kitchen counter, my eyes sweeping the family room, the bedroom, the door to the backyard. My outdoor storage unit catches my eye. The door isn't fully closed. It's an old door, sticky; you have to close it with intention. No one would have even noticed it was cracked open—no one except someone who had a five-year relationship with that door and knew what was hidden behind it.

I notice. I know.

"What have you taken today?"

John's eyes drift back to me, attempt to focus and meet my gaze, fail. He smiles at the sight of the food I've brought and attempts to sit up. Despite my tension, I breathe a little easier. He's conscious, at least.

We both know exactly what I'm referencing.

"It was too much, honey," he says. "The pain was too much."

His usual mantra.

"I found the lockbox, and I broke it open," he says. "I took the Percocet and Soma."

Now I begin to register the scene around him. His laptop is open in front of him, phone next to it, headphones tossed on the table, all of it surrounded by empty bottles of soda and water. He's clearly been working nonstop.

"How many did you take?"

"Oh . . . just three or four Percocet . . . and a couple Soma."

My stomach doesn't just drop. It hits the floor and shatters. I struggle to breathe. To gain perspective. This is a man with skin covered in scabs that crack open and bleed every time he moves, with gastrointestinal disturbance, with joints and muscles that ache. A man with a strange medical condition eating him up from the inside. But in this moment, my compassion is engulfed by a cortisol wave of fear and rage. *Overdose.*

I try to curb the bite in my voice. "When?"

He turns away from me, suddenly preoccupied with little Tinkerbell. Is it guilt or shame that flickers across his once undeniably handsome, now ruddy and scabbed face?

"I started looking for the lockbox after you left."

That was almost eight hours ago. What I was witnessing was the residual of a drug interaction that likely began six hours ago. Again, an unavoidable thought: *He could have died.*

Later I would count the pills in those locked away bottles—it was much more than "just three to four Percocet and a couple Soma."

To find that lockbox, John had to make his way through three separate locks. Behind that wonky door that led into the storage unit is a huge metal vault that had been left behind by the previous owners. There is only one key to that vault, which is on my key ring. Furthermore, the storage unit is also kept locked.

But John is a master of picking locks. In 2002, we attended DEF CON in Las Vegas, and there was a lock-picking exhibition. John proudly jostled through every single lock, no matter the difficulty. The man is Mensa-level smart, an engineer with a punk rock soul. Now, his intellect is abetting a life-threatening addiction.

From that afternoon on, I live in fear for his life. Still, I somehow tune out of the data staring me in the face. I trust his professed concern, equal to mine, about the medications that are being prescribed and the withdrawal effects we are noticing. I trust that when he gives me the pill bottles, he is giving me *all* the pill bottles. I trust the version of the man I loved who existed before the drugs. That man is the real John.

Am I naive? Hopeful? Idealistic? I am in love. And he really is sick.

I feel that acknowledging the elephant in the room means betraying him and us. Nevertheless, when John returns to his home in Los Angeles the next day, I reach out to Laura, one of my dearest friends from my graduate school program to ask if we can spend some time together. Though I trust her implicitly, I am terrified to say the words I need so desperately to speak aloud.

We stop to get gasoline and, while the pump runs, I turn to her from the passenger seat, inhale a shuddering breath, and spit the hateful words out.

"John is abusing pain medicine. I think he's addicted. I don't know what to do."

Amid the traitorous guilt, I feel some relief. I am so deeply and intensely alone within the situation; all I want is to break the pattern somehow. This may be a weak attempt, but I don't know what else to do. I don't think she knows what to do with it either. Neither of us mentions it again—until that fateful morning after his death when I blinked my eyes open and there she blessedly, heartbreakingly, was.

Without answers, John and I continue our dance. The cycle of addiction can be similar to the cycle of intimate partner violence: an instance of acting out followed by days of contrite behavior. He knows he screwed up big time, and in the days afterward, he is the "perfect" partner. The fights around his medication use disappear; no more begging for "just one extra pill because the pain is *really bad* today." He seems to know he is walking the edge of me doing something drastic to intervene.

Despite how much I desperately want to make him flush all the pills, there is no way I can force him to go cold turkey. When someone stops using opioids, they can experience severe and potentially life-threatening withdrawal symptoms that can lead to severe complications, such as dehydration, electrolyte imbalance, seizures, and respiratory arrest, all of which can be fatal (APA, 2013).

However, I do start accompanying him to doctor appointments. I have to make sure his doctors know he is abusing the pain medications. Of course, he takes it in stride, letting me voice my considerations and concerns and listening to how they plan to support him in being functional while managing his pain. (At the same time, he begins doctor-shopping in secret, something I won't find out about until months after his death.)

He also starts being much more amenable to conversations about treatment and the necessity of therapy. This creates a sense of hope within me, even though he pushes it all down the road: "After the wedding, Kitten. We don't have time right now."

He remains adamant that we not talk to our families about it, and my protective loyalty wins over my better judgment. Both our family systems are complicated, and his shame is so overwhelming that it feels like it would be more punitive than helpful to let anybody else know what was happening.

I choose to be alone with silence in order to honor him. After all, we have a plan to help him. I can see we are looking over the edge of a precipice, but I want to be there with him. I tell myself that with my silence, I am slowly backing us both away from it.

I was wrong.

CHAPTER 8

Premonition and Ultimatum

"Men are not prisoners of fate, but only
prisoners of their own minds."

—Franklin D. Roosevelt

In the weeks that follow the incident with Tinkerbell, John begrudgingly agrees that after the wedding, he will start looking into treatment options. In deference to his shame, I won't tell his family. We still have details to iron out, but I am breathing a little easier. I had won a significant battle. I knew for him the war to sobriety was to come. I never imagined it would go nuclear.

Just a week before the tragedy, we are coming home from my parents' house in Palm Desert. It has been the perfect weekend: dinners with family friends, wedding planning, the dress fitting, buying the veil. One of my mother's dear friends slips me a little white silky something—"for the honeymoon," she winks at me over a glass of champagne. Outwardly, I grin and we clink our glasses. Inside, I struggle to accept that John's pain means there will be no traditional wedding night for us.

John sits with the guys, slightly out of place in his Tommy Bahama silk button-down and oversized cotton khakis, the only two fabrics that don't cause his skin to burn. In a way, it's just as well—his usual punk rock T-shirts don't fly with my parents' crew. He catches my eye and blows me a kiss. His grin is still contagious in spite of it all.

We sing along to the band Postal Service on the drive home, telling stories of the weekend, planning the week ahead. I carefully engineer our conversation to stay light so as not to veer into the tense territory of his physical or emotional health. Through the windshield, I spy the green swirl of the Green Burrito sign.

"Hungry?"

"Absolutely. Let's get our burritos."

A funny sentiment: *our burritos.* Couples have such interesting traditions.

I navigate to the right lane and signal to exit onto CA-243 when he speaks up.

"You know I'm going to die young."

My stomach drops and ice-cold fear unfurls inside me. I struggle to calm my rapid heartbeat by taking slow and deep breaths.

I start chanting in my head: *Do not react, Kate, do not react.* I pull over on the freeway ramp and stop the car.

He turns to me, surprised. "What are you doing?"

I pin him with my gaze, struggling to keep my voice from shaking.

"We're getting married in two weeks. What on earth are you talking about?!"

Every alarm bell in my brain is going off. My hands are pulsing on the steering wheel. The image of him sprawled on my sofa, head lolled to the side with that terrifying blank stare slams into my brain. I taste bile in my throat.

"I've always known that I'm somebody who is going to die young," he replies casually. "And you will find great love and you will have to. You have to find great love again, and I'll always be with you. And when you find that person, I'll let you know."

This conversation is a big part of what kept me going through the trials that were to come. But sitting on that freeway on-ramp, I don't know that they're about to begin in less than one week. Instead, I regress to an angry thirteen-year-old.

"Shut up!" I growl. "I'm dying before you, and you'll be lonely for the rest of your life after I die because you will never find a love like ours again!"

I am angry, and at the core of that anger is the deep truth of my fear. I am more scared by his certainty than I would be if he were suicidal. He looks at me, puts his hand on mine, smiles his knowing smile. It is usually comforting, but this time it makes the pit in my stomach, an ever-present companion over the previous eighteen months, yawn open as deep as the Grand Canyon.

By the time we get home, I have transcended my emotions into assertive certainty.

"You're going into treatment immediately," I say. "You're not going to die. Not on my watch."

Terrified but resolute, I slide my engagement ring off my finger, a place it had sat for almost two years while I completed graduate school, and place it firmly on the counter in front of him.

"This is your choice," I say. "You can walk out the door and this is over. If you stay, we're not going on our honeymoon after the wedding—you're going into treatment instead. We don't have to tell anyone, but there's no longer any other option."

He looks at the ring. He looks at my face. And then he leaves.

My world goes black. I hear the front door slam behind him and his car rev out of the driveway. *He's gone.* My legs give out beneath me, and I hit the stone floor with enough noise to startle my dogs awake. They come to me and lick my face as I lie curled on the floor, dry heaving with tears streaming down my face, looking up at the ring on the counter, repeating the truth that I could not believe: "He left."

But then he comes back. He walks in the door and says something I will never forget: "I couldn't bear you believing in me and being disappointed."

Less than one week later, the evening of June 13, he would drop me off at his little sister's apartment and we will say our goodbyes forever.

CHAPTER 9

Not All Emotional Experiences Are Created Equal

"Ultimately, traumatization is about being trapped in the uncompleted act of escape."

—Ronald A. Ruden

When people think of "trauma," they often think of PTSD, a concept usually associated with surviving war, natural disasters, rape, multicar pileups, a global pandemic such as COVID-19, and similar disastrous events. In truth, trauma doesn't only manifest from the types of experiences that earn headlines on the evening news. There are many sources of trauma, big and small—from a devastating miscarriage within the first weeks of pregnancy, to the loss of one's job, to the neglect one experienced as a child. It can result from any perceived threat to our sense of ourselves, our attachment, and our connection to the world around us. Luckily, not all traumatic events are created equal, and our brains have evolved finely tuned mechanisms to help us successfully process many of the painful and difficult things that we encounter in life (McEwen, 2019; Spencer-Segal & Akil, 2019).

Traumatic stress, a manifestation of experiencing a traumatic event, occurs when there is a highly stressful and emotional event that results in the brain shifting into a very particular electrochemical state. In a moment of traumatic stress, the brain jumps into hyperdrive. While Amy the amygdala is activated to assess the situation for safety and escape, other brain areas begin furiously making sense of the incoming data in order to find the greatest possibilities for our survival.

Luckily, experiencing traumatic stress does not always mean our brains will encode the event and its impact forever. In fact, only 6 to 8 percent of people exposed to a traumatic experience will develop PTSD (Goldstein et al., 2016; Pietrzak et al., 2011). That being said, the impact of being exposed to trauma without adequate support for the mind and body to process it can be life-altering. For example, research indicates that 70 percent of patients with recurrent depression have four or more traumatically encoded memories (Kessler et al., 1995).

So what causes an event to be traumatically encoded in some brains but not others? And why are some brains more susceptible to encoding trauma than others? Dr. Ronald Ruden, the founder of the Havening Techniques®, created an acronym to identify the critical criteria for a trauma encoding: EMLI. The acronym stands for *Event*, *Meaning*, *Landscape*, and *Inescapability* (Ruden, 2011; 2018).

Event

First, there is the traumatic *Event*—an experience that produces intense emotions. We can experience an Event in three different ways:

1. Firsthand involvement (the Event happens to us)
2. Secondhand (we witness the Event happening)

3. Thirdhand (we hear about the Event happening; this is also known as vicarious/secondary traumatization)

In my case, we might identify the Event as me rushing up to the apartment door, pounding on it, hearing the dogs bark, but seeing and hearing no response from John. However, I would say the Event began when John did not pick up the phone on the first call and, despite feeling uneasy, I made the decision to ignore my instincts and go back with the sisters to Manhattan Beach for a little more revelry. I admit that freaking out at that moment would seem unreasonable to an outsider; it certainly did to his sisters. But it was more than intuition—I had information about John's physical and mental condition they did not have. Later, as I willed the taxi driver to go faster, my heart raced, my adrenaline spiked repeatedly, and my thoughts were spinning, irrational, incongruent. This was all before I even began the mad rush to the locked door. Then there was the crescendo of this Event: my panicked shriek as I managed to break the door open. This led into an agonizing scene that remained locked in my brain for five years: my futile attempts to make him breathe. All of this together created the Event.

The alertness we experience in the Event is the result of this hyper-speed processing in our most primal brain areas (Oya et al., 2002; Sato et al., 2011). The choices we make in these moments are driven by hardwired neurobiological survival reactions.

Meaning

After the Event comes the *Meaning* we extract from it. Our brains are constantly making Meaning out of our experiences and interactions, an instinct that arises from our deep human need to have a cohesive narrative about our lives. Remember that storytelling plays a critical role in how we understand the world and ourselves within it. The extraction of Meaning is so important that in as little as a quarter of a second, our previous experiences, emotions, memories, and senses begin to determine how our brains interpret the present moment, driven by those learned core values around safety, lovability, belonging, and success.

The Meaning our brains make out of the world around us plays a significant role in how our brains and bodies react in a situation. My Event of having John suddenly ripped from my life most definitely threatened my sense of Self, my attachment, and my greatest connection to the world. Our lives had been extraordinarily integrated, commingled to such a degree that it almost felt like there wasn't a me without him. On that fateful evening of his death, as I listened to the distant sound of sirens coming closer, the Meaning my brain started to weave around that experience was that *I should have known better.* I had failed John by not immediately coming home after that first unanswered call.

Landscape

The Event and Meaning play out in the context of the underlying *Landscape* of our brains—that is, the electrochemical state of the brain at any given moment. (An everyday example of Landscape is when you get "hangry"—so hungry and low on blood sugar that you become extra reactive to stressors.) As we learned in chapter 5, 90 percent of the input to the thinking brain comes from internal processing (our past experiences, emotions, memories, and senses interpreting present reality) rather than from external stimuli. In a moment where our survival is (or feels) in jeopardy, that 90 percent is heavily influenced by the amygdala's core drive to keep us safe.

The brain's Landscape is also influenced by the developmental experiences of our lives—moments of joy and celebration, feeling safe and loved, experiences of stress, pain, or illness, as well as traumatically encoded experiences that occurred before the age of eighteen (the ACEs we discussed in chapter 3). While our systems are designed to adapt to stress, there is significant information showing that when we are exposed to chronic stress or trauma in childhood, the systems may be, as van der Kolk (2014) writes, "reset to interpret the world as a dangerous place." This reset can have long-term costs and, as you'll learn, literally rewire the brain (for review, see McEwen & Akil, 2020; van der Kolk, 2014).

As you know, I experienced my share of ACEs growing up and went on to struggle profoundly under their influence, particularly during times of stress. Living in the chronic stress of John's illness and growing addiction combined with the recent Event of John partially OD'ing made my brain's landscape even more vulnerable. As a result, the Event of John's death and the Meaning my brain made of it were running their course on a Landscape that was fertile ground for future pain and suffering.

Inescapability

Inescapability is the final variable. The extent to which a person feels they have agency during a traumatic or stressful event plays a critical role in how the brain processes the Event (Seligman, 1975). It doesn't matter whether the Event is really Inescapable or simply perceived that way; if the brain believes that we are unable to escape a stressful or traumatic event, then the traumatic encoding will occur.

It is vital to note that the experience of something being *Inescapable* does not have to reach conscious awareness. Even if I had arrived in time to successfully resuscitate John, I still may have suffered deeply encoded trauma from this event. It is the *possibility* of not escaping that makes the difference in traumatic encoding. The point at which the Event became Inescapable for me was when I began the slow walk back to the apartment. The moment it hit me that John could not be saved, the Event and its Meaning became firmly encoded in the tortured Landscape of my brain.

The brain is wired first and foremost to process information through a threat assessment in order to protect our survival (Rozin & Royzman 2001). For trauma survivors, this threat assessment may become a lens through which the brain interprets life. Once an Event warranting a threat assessment occurs, Amy lights up and guides the brain's information process through a rapid-fire electro-chemical assessment:

- What is the *Meaning*? Is your safety, worth, or connection to your community threatened in any way?

- What is your overarching brain *Landscape*? Are you anxious? Frantic? Burned out? Calm?

- Is the situation *Inescapable* or do you perceive some way out?

If your brain assesses that the incoming flood of sensory data is threatening enough to your survival, your brain will create a traumatic memory. From the moment an encoding occurs in the brain, it will play a starring role in how your brain and body make sense of the world around you for a lifetime to come. After the moment of encoding, the traumatized brain and body are always prepared to react to any stimulus that reminds them of the original threat (Corchs & Schiller, 2019), even to the point of complete physical depletion. In short, the past becomes the lens through which the brain understands the present.

The Impact of EMLIs

Take a moment to reflect on the meaning of a cough back in November 2019: a tickle in your throat, allergies, a head cold, or maybe the onset of a flu. Now think about the meaning of a cough in April 2020, when the coronavirus pandemic was on the rise. By then, a cough meant the possible onset of a virus that could kill you or your loved ones. Even now, those who survived the worst stages of the COVID-19 pandemic time may find their Amy still jumps to attention when someone across the room sneezes or coughs. Our brains have learned a new meaning for these experiences.

In every moment, our incredible brains are noting, assessing, and learning in order to keep us alive and safe. But Amy is not able to decipher the difference between Events that pose an actual survival threat and Events that are simply reminders of the past. Moreover, the more vulnerable your Landscape is, the greater the role past EMLIs play in how Amy defines your present-day life. When a present-day Event reminds Amy of EMLIs from your past, Amy guides your thinking brain to project past moments of fear, threat, anxiety, rage, anger, et cetera into your present experience. For some of us, this causes such disruption that we begin living in the throes of PTSD. The diagnostic criteria for PTSD (APA, 2013) reads like a checklist of my symptoms for five years after John's death:

Posttraumatic Stress Disorder: Code 309.81

A. Exposure to actual or threatened death, serious injury, or sexual violence in one (or more) of the following ways:

1. Directly experiencing the traumatic event(s). - *Check!*

2. Witnessing, in person, the event(s) as it occurred to others. - *Check!*

3. Learning that the traumatic event(s) occurred to a close family member or close friend. In cases of actual or threatened death of a family member or friend, the event(s) must have been violent or accidental. – *Check!*

4. Experiencing repeated or extreme exposure to aversive details of the traumatic event(s) (e.g., first responders collecting human remains; police officers repeatedly exposed to details of child abuse). – *Check!*

B. Presence of one (or more) of the following intrusion symptoms associated with the traumatic event(s), beginning after the traumatic event(s) occurred:

1. Recurrent, involuntary, and intrusive distressing memories of the traumatic event(s). – *Check!*

2. Recurrent distressing dreams in which the content and/or affect of the dream are related to the traumatic event(s). – *Check!*

3. Dissociative reactions (e.g., flashbacks) in which the individual feels or acts as if the traumatic event(s) were recurring. (Such reactions may occur on a continuum, with the most extreme expression being a complete loss of awareness of present surroundings.) – *Check!*

4. Intense or prolonged psychological distress at exposure to internal or external cues that symbolize or resemble an aspect of the traumatic event(s). – *Check!*

5. Marked physiological reactions to internal or external cues that symbolize or resemble an aspect of the traumatic event(s). – *Check!*

C. Persistent avoidance of stimuli associated with the traumatic event(s), beginning after the traumatic event(s) occurred, as evidenced by one or both of the following:

  1. Avoidance of or efforts to avoid distressing memories, thoughts, or feelings about or closely associated with the traumatic event(s). – *Check!*

  2. Avoidance of or efforts to avoid external reminders (people, places, conversations, activities, objects, situations) that arouse distressing memories, thoughts, or feelings about or closely associated with the traumatic event(s). – *Check!*

D. Negative alterations in cognitions and mood associated with the traumatic event(s), beginning or worsening after the traumatic event(s) occurred, as evidenced by two (or more) of the following:

  1. Inability to remember an important aspect of the traumatic event(s) (typically due to dissociative amnesia, and not to other factors such as head injury, alcohol, or drugs). – *I wish!*

  2. Persistent and exaggerated negative beliefs or expectations about oneself, others, or the world (e.g., "I am bad," "No one can be trusted," "The world is completely dangerous," "My whole nervous system is permanently ruined"). – *Check!*

  3. Persistent, distorted cognitions about the cause or consequences of the traumatic event(s) that lead the individual to blame himself/herself or others. – *Check!*

  4. Persistent negative emotional state (e.g., fear, horror, anger, guilt, or shame). – *Check!*

5. Markedly diminished interest or participation in significant activities. – *Check!*

6. Feelings of detachment or estrangement from others. – *Check!*

7. Persistent inability to experience positive emotions (e.g., inability to experience happiness, satisfaction, or loving feelings). – *Luckily, no.*

E. Marked alterations in arousal and reactivity associated with the traumatic event(s), beginning or worsening after the traumatic event(s) occurred, as evidenced by two (or more) of the following:

1. Irritable behavior and angry outbursts (with little or no provocation), typically expressed as verbal or physical aggression toward people or objects. – *Luckily, no.*

2. Reckless or self-destructive behavior. – *Overt behaviors, no. Thoughts, yes.*

3. Hypervigilance. – *Check!*

4. Exaggerated startle response. – *Check!*

5. Problems with concentration. – *Check!*

6. Sleep disturbance (e.g., difficulty falling or staying asleep or restless sleep). – *Check!*

F. Duration of the disturbance (Criteria B, C, D and E) is more than 1 month. – *How's five years?*

G. The disturbance causes clinically significant distress or impairment in social, occupational, or other important areas of functioning. – *Check!*

H. The disturbance is not attributable to the physiological effects of a substance (e.g., medication, alcohol) or another medical condition. – *Check!*

Notice how the symptoms of PTSD make sense when we consider them as the brain working diligently to keep us safe from stimuli that have harmed us in the past? Furthermore, because the amygdala's primary goal is to keep us alive, we'll never catch her sleeping on the job. This means that stimuli encoded at the time of the traumatic experience(s) can also creep into our sleep. There is no break when the brain believes we are in danger.

That vigilance in our brains is one of the keys to our survival, with or without PTSD. But as you can see from the criteria above, that can come at a great cost in terms of quality of life. Still, there is hope. Some of the elements in our brain/body systems that set us up for being hijacked by trauma are the very same things that can help us find our way out of it.

Until recently, much of the foundational Landscape of the brain was considered to be hardwired based on the encoded experiences of the past. A good childhood meant a good life, while an unfortunate childhood meant a greater likelihood for a traumatic life. What devastating news for the great number of people who have experienced ACEs! Fortunately, this is no longer seen as a given. We now know that we have the ability to heal and create an abundant and healthy neuro-landscape. My own survival story, and the thousands of stories I have witnessed, are testimony to this fact.

Bottom line, our brains can change. We have the opportunity to create new outcomes, new ways forward, for our brains and ultimately ourselves. This is the power of neuroplasticity, and we will explore that in greater depth in the next two chapters.

CHAPTER 10

How the Past Defines the Present

"In PTSD a traumatic event is not remembered and relegated to one's past in the same way as other life events. Trauma continues to intrude with visual, auditory, and/or other somatic reality on the lives of its victims. Again and again, they relive the life-threatening experiences they suffered, reacting in mind and body as though such events were still occurring. PTSD is a complex psychobiological condition."

—Babette Rothschild

One of the most complicated parts of a traumatic experience, both for survivors and those caring for them, is wrapping our minds around the fact that each experience of trauma is by nature unique. The consequences of a traumatic experience are different for every single individual involved, even those who have suffered the same traumatic experience. For one individual in a car accident, the Event might be the moment of impact. For another, it may be the moment they realize they can't escape from the car.

Once a traumatic experience has occurred, the brain gets to work identifying related or similar data and weaving it all into a fabric of information that will overlay our perspectives going forward. Like Spiderman shooting webs from his hands as he swings from building to building, the brain goes on grabbing any information or insight it can draw from each new experience and weaves it into the narrative that promises to keep us safe.

The brain also navigates back across our lives, looking for past similar experiences to reinforce the narrative—remember that 90 percent of the present is defined by the past. It weaves in our thoughts and feelings, how our bodies respond to stimuli and how we interpret those responses, as well as a vast array of external sensory data—where were we in the moment of the trauma? What did we hear and see? Was there a smell in the air? A taste in our mouths?

The result is a complex array of dramatic changes in how we interpret present-day experiences and the world around us. We call this *building the trauma filter*. To understand it better, let's first examine the variables that the brain may encode in a moment of traumatic encoding: *threatening content, complex content,* and *contextual cues* (Ruden, 2011; 2018).

Threatening Content: The Experience, Real or Perceived, That Presents a Threat to Survival

As we learned in the last chapter, Amy is always filtering incoming information and assessing for threat. Some types of threat are inherent to our species; in other words, we are born into the world already being wary of some types of stimuli. For example, in a groundbreaking study, Eleanor Gibson and Richard Walk (1960) examined depth perception in infants. What they found is that infants were reluctant to move across variations of "cliffs" even when being called to by their primary caregivers. This was fascinating because children typically use their caregivers to help identify what is and is not safe. The fact that these young children refused to go across the experimental "cliffs" means that there was a survival instinct overriding their urge to go to their caregivers. The study has since been replicated with numerous other mammals, and the consensus is that as soon as a mammal is able to move about, it will avoid anything that looks or feels like a sharp drop. Before we've ever been outside our own homes, we know that falling off cliffs can kill.

Just out of curiosity, how do you feel about roller coasters? Don't worry, there's no right answer. I find this topic to be a fascinating example of how different brains process threat. If you dislike roller coasters, your survival brain has done its job in keeping you out of a metal box that is plummeting toward the earth at 80+ miles an hour.* If you love roller coasters, your brain has created a different meaning around the experience and feels exhilaration instead. Anxiety and excitement are remarkably similar in terms of their electrochemical presentation in the brain. It's the way we think about the feeling that makes the difference (Brooks, 2014; Jamieson et al., 2012).

Our brains have designed an internal safety mechanism around anything that killed enough of our ancestors for evolution to take note. These mechanisms are called *unconditioned threat stimuli*. In addition to roller coasters, some other examples of stimuli our brains are inherently designed to be wary of are creepy crawlies, things that go bump in the night, suffocating spaces, and

---

* The Formula Rossa rollercoaster located at Ferrari World features a maximum speed of 149 miles per hour. Yikes! Or, yay!?

unexpected loud noises. Indiana Jones's survival brain was certainly on-point when those snakes showed up in *Raiders of the Lost Ark*. While we may not have any personal life experiences with threatening content like venomous insects or the deprivation of light or air, unconditioned threat stimuli make us innately aware of the danger they present.

On the other hand, some types of threatening content are learned through stressful or traumatic life experiences. The memory encoding in these experiences creates conditioned threat stimuli, new safety mechanisms the brain constantly builds into an innate threat template in order to keep us alive (for review, see LeDoux, 2012).

For example, I have a vivid memory of being a child and rushing across a parking lot in Denver, Colorado, toward the craft store Michael's. I was so overtaken by excitement about the possibility of new stickers that I was oblivious to the huge machines on wheels navigating the parking lot. Suddenly my arm snapped back and I was lifted high into the air, tiny feet dangling, as my mother's shriek "Katy!" filled the air. A silver car glided by, narrowly avoiding my fluttering kicks. Setting me back on my feet, my mom grasped my arms in her hands; her face hovered over mine, usually kind but now red and mottled as her fear transformed into anger. "Do not run off," she said in a tight "this is serious" voice. "Pay attention. You could have been killed!"

While this experience was not traumatic, I vividly remember the intensity on her face, the fear I felt at that initial "Katy!", and her finger pointing at the now parked silver sedan. All these sensory details left an important imprint on Amy that she now utilizes to ensure my safety around cars.

Complex Content: Surrounding Information That Does Not Present a Threat in Itself, but Is Connected to the Threatening Content

When it comes to a stressful or traumatic experience, not all data is created equal. Trauma stimuli—the actual threats to our safety—are the warning sirens of traumatically encoded experiences. Been in a car accident? It's logical that you would have an anxiety response to screeching tires or prefer side streets over major roads. Less understandable, however, would be the fear of riding on a train. Those less logical trauma reactions are the result of what is known as *complex content,* also known as facilitated threat generalization (Corchs & Schiller, 2019), which refers to all other data the brain picks up in a moment of a trauma, such as what your body was experiencing and what you were thinking, noticing, and feeling (Baratta et al., 2007; Lissek et al., 2005; Ruden, 2018). All this data comes together to build the CASE (more on this acronym in the next chapter) the brain uses to ensure our future safety.

Contextual Cues: The Environment Around You at the Time of a Traumatic Encoding

We've talked about how one of the brain's safety features is making meaning out of the traumatic experiences we go through. It does the same thing with activations associated with the trauma. This is where the *contextual cues* come in. Your brain reads danger into what was happening in the environment around you when the threatening content showed up. Anytime you become aware of those cues—the intersection where a car accident occurred, the date of a shattering break-up with a loved one, "sundowner" syndrome for people who struggle with addictive drinking—your brain signals *danger* (Corchs & Schiller, 2019; Ruden, 2018)! In my case, the wedding that became the funeral was a landmine of contextual cues. Being surrounded by all the beautiful ceremony details we'd carefully planned together—the same flowers, the same romantic selections from Beethoven and Bright Eyes, even the same guests— turned my experience of sorrow into a fresh hell of suffering.

Even in the most mundane experience, the brain is constantly sorting through and processing the clues offered by our environments. This is called *contextual integration*, and it supports a detailed encoding of present moment stimuli that helps us accurately and appropriately recall the experience later (Ehlers & Clark, 2000). Moreover, it utilizes all past experiences to enhance processing speed in the present. For example, if you can imagine walking into your local grocery store and you know exactly where to find the produce section, the checkout stands, and the bread aisle, that is because of contextual integration. This function is also critical in helping the brain build a cohesive narrative—the before, during, and after—of any life experience.

However, trauma changes the brain's experience of that encoding moment. In a moment when your survival is (or feels) threatened, your brain begins encoding a host of external and internal stimuli to draw upon at a future date. Rather than simply focusing on the threatening content like a poisonous snake, a speeding car, or a raised fist, Amy weaves in details like the spark of curiosity that led you off the hiking trail, the chatter of your kids in the car seat behind you, or the feeling of being stared at by a crowd of onlookers right before the bully punched you.

As we've discussed, survival requires us to react rapidly, and the amygdala's hijack takes precedence over the brain's ability to integrate context in processing the information we're getting in the moment of the trauma. In trauma, the brain locks us into the amygdala's experience so that we repeatedly live it out in our minds—not to torture us, but to help us find an escape. In other words, we're reliving the trauma so that we can avoid or escape it if it shows up again.

Whether the trauma is an ACE or an experience encoded later in life, it goes beyond impacting the amygdala to reshape the way our brains utilize and process information, our sense of Self, and even our bodies. Moreover, since Amy also uses reminders from the past to keep us safe in the present, she may also cast a wider attentional net for all data (threatening content, complex content, contextual cues) that can be linked to the traumatic Event. The brain is always building its library of what it believes to be the most critical information for keeping you safe, and the "extra" information of complex content serves as warning signs of possible threats in the future. The side effects of this can be extremely confusing at best and downright terrifying at worst. For those of us who have survived trauma, these unexpected and often unknown encodings can become sensory cues that throw us into an emotional loop. I think of them as sleeper cell trauma grenades, just waiting for the perfect moment to go off.

Until I was able to fully process the traumatic encodings within the EMLI of John's death, I had numerous trauma grenades following me around. Some I was aware of and could manage. Others were hidden from me in the deep recesses of my amygdala, waiting to explode.

***

Flash forward to 2013. John has been gone for almost four years. In the time since, my life has been carefully redesigned to reduce exposure to trauma while empowering my unique version of normalcy. No more spontaneity, lots of highly controlled structure.

But when a couple of friends offer me a ticket to a comedy show in Hollywood, I agree to go along in an attempt to be a "normal" person again. Laughter is great for the brain—what could go wrong?

The show's first act is fabulously hilarious. The curtain falls. My friends and I chat during the brief intermission. Then, as the house lights go down for Act Two, I turn my attention back to the stage just as the curtain rises to reveal a body on the floor covered in a white sheet.

My heartbeat accelerates. My palms start to sweat. Amy's considering her options—*Is this a threat? Do we panic?*

Before I know what's happening, an actor runs onto the stage, grabs the prone body's foot and drags the body across the floor. An image intrudes before me: John's body being callously pulled along by the oblivious EMT. On stage, the sheet gets caught and the "dead body" springs to life, yelling—no doubt something ridiculous and brilliant—but I don't hear the words. As the crowd bursts into laughter, I shove my fist in my mouth and bite down hard. It's all I can do to contain my scream.

NO! NO! NO! Not here! Not now!

Dear Amy comes to the rescue with a coughing fit. My chest feels like it's collapsing in on itself. The skit has moved on, but Amy still has me paralyzed, half-suffocating. The past whispers in my ear: *I can't make him breathe.*

Fighting panic, I bolt, likely trampling people's feet as I stumble through the aisle, out of the theater, down the stairs. Half coughing, half choking, I collapse in the street, sobbing.

It's a Saturday night in Hollywood. People are flowing around me, stopping to stare. One of the theater employees hovers just inside the door, a wary eye on me. The panic in my chest gives way to a swell of shame and embarrassment as my conscious brain registers how undeniably "crazy" I look, how "broken" I am.

Kate, breathe! I remind myself, but it only results in a new onslaught of sobs. That whisper from the past returns: *I can't make him breathe!*

Eventually, the theater employee musters the courage to approach me and inquire if I need help. The fear on her face pushes my thinking brain back online; my core value for caretaking is very powerful. I manage a deep, shaky breath, ask her for a tissue, and offer her a blunt account of what happened: "I had a flashback related to the dead body part of the show."

Total transparency is my new way of managing social relationships—it helps shocked onlookers normalize what they're witnessing. Sometimes I wish I had a card I could hand out in the wake of insane reactions like these: "My name is Kate; I have PTSD. Don't mind me."

"I'm sorry," I tell the theater employee, "I'm okay. Are there other dead bodies in the third act?"

This is another tactic I've used extensively in these situations. Giving the concerned person a job to do to support helps deflect from the trauma behavior.

She smiles at me kindly and hands over a tissue. "Nope, the next act has some humans acting like dogs. Is that okay for you?"

I stand, brush off the street from my jeans, and swipe at my nose, matching her smile. "Thank you," I say. "Humans being dogs are fine."

She directs me toward the restroom, then invites me to wait in the lobby until the second act wraps up. I buy a bottle of water from her, complete with a $40 tip, and return to the show.

As this story shows, who you are or what you know has no bearing on the impact trauma has on you. I am a trauma specialist. I've spent years studying these effects on the brain and body. Even as this flashback and very public panic attack were happening, I knew what my brain was doing and why, but my "knowing brain" was turned off while the experience was underway. In that moment, Amy was fully in charge, and the only thing that mattered to her was the threat to my survival represented by the body on that stage.

Anyone who has ever had an experience like this also knows the shame and embarrassment that engulfs the mind once the trauma reaction subsides. It would be a long time before I would attend another show—that moment of hyperreactivity had given Amy a new set of data to tie into the threat narrative.

In the days following, my mind played through a million different scenarios where my scream wasn't muffled by the uproarious laughter of the crowd. From months afterward, just the idea of going to the theater would activate a fluttering of panic in my chest. The network of fear and avoidance that Amy builds on top of the original traumas means that the world gets progressively smaller and smaller (Horowitz, 2011).

The comedy show was a perfect storm of sensory activations for my encoded complex content. The sheet-covered body on the stage presented a perverse parallel to my real-life experience, launching the same cascade of physiological responses that occurred when I saw John's body covered in that white sheet and dragged across the floor. The result: a brand-new traumatically encoded experience. The *threatening content* was public humiliation, the barely contained scream, feeling out of control, being seen as "crazy" by friends and colleagues. The *complex content* was the sensory activation of the actor's body covered with a white sheet, intensified by the grabbing and dragging and the crowded space around me. The *contextual cues* were the general atmosphere of uncertainty—*What could be coming next?*

Now that we understand what is happening with outside stimuli when trauma is encoded, let's look at what is happening deep within the brain in the moment of encoding. Recall from chapter 5 that 90 percent of each present moment is defined by experiences from our pasts. If only 10 percent of the present moment is being created by the sensory information within that moment, how does that 90 percent of learned experiences guide the outcome?

CHAPTER 11

When the Brain Makes a CASE

"Do I contradict myself? Very well then I contradict myself, (I am large, I contain multitudes.)"

—Walt Whitman

Only 100 years ago, the scientific community believed that the brain was mainly a storage system, a "black box" where the data of an experience and how it impacted us was kept for life. Even after we came to understand that brains develop through childhood and young adulthood and remain very flexible into a person's mid-twenties, our concept was still that the brain became rigid and unchangeable after the age of twenty-five or so.

In the past thirty years, however, neurobiology research has shown that our brains are *plastic* (i.e., capable of change) throughout our lives. It is true that the brains of children are more plastic than those of adults (which explains why what we learn in childhood can be so formative to our sense of Self) and that the brain's ability to change slows down in adulthood (which explains why changing what we've learned about ourselves in childhood can be so challenging). But the brain remains able to change and adapt even as we get older. Anyone who has taught their grandma how to use a smartphone has seen this process in action.

The brain's ability to change is known as *neuroplasticity*, and it works by forming new connections among the brain's roughly 86.1 billion neurons (von Bartheld et al., 2016). The human brain is in a never-ending state of construction, building new information pathways and linking them to each other while also demolishing old pathways that are no longer needed. These connections are constantly changing and reorganizing, creating the neurological basis for the behaviors, beliefs, and memories that help mold our lives and, ultimately, our sense of Self (for review, see Mateos-Aparicio & Rodríguez-Moreno, 2019).

There are two sides to neuroplasticity. On the one hand, neuroplasticity empowers us with the opportunity to intentionally help the brain build new connections—what I call "neural freeways"—that help us explore and learn new things in the world. It also empowers us to heal from stress, anxiety, trauma, and more. On the other hand, there is neuroplasticity's darker side, known as *stress-induced structural plasticity* (Vyas et al., 2002, 2006; Wang et al., 2017). In the wake of something chronically stressful or traumatic, such as an EMLI, the brain applies its incredible adaptation capacity to our survival. Specifically, it builds neural freeways that take us to places we would rather not go but where Amy believes we will be safe.

Stress-induced structural plasticity (SISP) starts to build during and after moments of deep stress. It develops out of direct connections between the amygdala and your predominant memory centers, most notably your hippocampus. In these moments, Amy uses her senses to tune into and remember all the complex content and contextual cues within the situation—everything that you were seeing, smelling, hearing, tasting, and touching, and where you were in relation to it all. At the same time, Amy is also recording what is happening within your emotions, thoughts, and body. Even pieces of data that may not seem inherently traumatic on the surface (like a white sheet draped over a body) get looped in if Amy senses they could help you survive this situation and avoid similar situations in the future.

Brain development and neuroplasticity, including SISP, are heavily informed by the core values of the amygdala: how we stay safe, are lovable and belong, and create success. These values align with our mind-body system's fundamental motivation to stay alive. In fact, the amygdala shows greater activity when our decisions and behaviors reward us for, in essence, not dying; that reward may be anything from a pat on the back for a job well done to successful evasion of physical and emotional pain in a difficult moment (Janak & Tye, 2015; Seymour et al., 2007). These reward experiences build the *CASE* for Self—that is, how we experience ourselves, others, and the world around us (Ruden, 2011; Truitt, 2022).

CASE is an acronym for four critical ways that the brain builds neural freeways around our internal experiences of the world:

- **Cognition:** What we think about the Self and Self in the world and the labels we assign to those thoughts that shape how we see and bear witness to the world, such as *smart/stupid, worthy/not good enough*, or *strong/weak*

- **Autonomic nervous system functioning and regulation:** Biological and physiological responses we don't have to think about, like heartbeat, blood pressure, and digestion

- **Somatosensory experiences:** Implicit memory, pain, felt sense/body memories, interoception (the felt sense of what's happening inside our bodies, such as brain fog or heartache)

- **Emotional affective responses:** All feelings and their physiological cues, positive or negative, related to our experiences, such as feeling proud when we win a game or feeling let down when a friend forgets our birthday

Your brain's unique CASE consists of all the experiences you have had throughout your life that have shaped your perception of the world. It molds your sense of Self and seamlessly guides your reactions and behaviors, consciously and unconsciously, in keeping with the amygdala's core values. Trauma or no trauma, Amy is always involved in constructing our CASE of the world around us.

The problem arises when, rather than seeing the world through a clear lens, Amy starts to experience the world with "stress glasses" on. When this happens, Amy starts to overwork, and SISP is likely to start guiding the way our brains make sense of the world. This is when Amy changes her approach—the guiding force for her CASE for Self is reduced to pain avoidance. We call this a CASE for survival (Ruden, 2011; Truitt, 2022). This shift in approach prompts our systems to pile on the stress hormones and can even impact our working memory, prioritizing the stress-related stimuli to serve up a CASE that presents a biased view of the world. We lose sight of the fact that there are moments of safety within every day and instead see the world as a yawning chasm of darkness and fear, waiting to swallow us whole if we don't keep our guards up.

The CASE for survival, or even trauma, may present something like this:

- **Cognition:** Labels like *Not good enough, Loser, Too intense,* or my personal go-tos, *Crazy and broken*

- **Autonomic nervous system function:** Rapid heart rate, impaired breathing, sweaty palms, migraine, TMJ (jaw clenching), or tingling

- **Somatosensory experience:** Heartache, pit in the stomach, "zoning out," or brain fog

- **Emotional affective response:** Shame, fear, anger, guilt, embarrassment, rage, disappointment, or jealousy

Like a good lawyer, Amy will build an exhaustive CASE around painful experiences to ensure the brain's ability to live safely afterward. The brain is extremely good at linking all these data points together so that it knows what they mean and how we should react. Unfortunately, these linkages do not always make us feel good, powerful, or secure.

For example, suppose the brain forms a neural freeway based on the Cognition *loser*. It might link together the Emotion of embarrassment and the Autonomic and Somatosensory feeling of an elevated heartbeat and strengthen those elements with sense memories of similar feelings you experienced in the past. Later on, whenever those CASE elements show up, the brain will be prepared (at an unconscious level) to react in self-protection.

Moreover, because Amy's CASE-informed survival strategies are anchored in the EMLI encodings of the past, they often neglect the crucial data that the trauma is no longer occurring in the present moment. As a result, you may react to common, everyday challenges as though they are the same type of pain, distress, or trauma you've experienced before. A prime example of this occurred to me two years after John's death. Despite being deep in my journey through complex grief and PTSD, I had signed up for eHarmony (at my friends' urging) and was trying to date again. As Adam and I parted ways after dinner, I casually asked that he text me when he got home to let me know he was okay. Less than an hour later, I had checked my Blackberry at least thirty times. No text message. No missed call. Nothing. Anxiety churned in my chest, a red-hot tightness clenching my shoulders.

Days later, I would bemoan my lack of second dates to my friends, only to have them clue me into the fact that it's less than ideal to conclude a first date with motherly behavior like asking for a "got home safe" text. But as of that day, I had not yet learned that lesson, and my amygdala's fear-generating narrative held a powerful grip on my thinking brain.

An hour and fifteen minutes passed. *He should definitely be home!* Unable to quell my growing anxiety, I picked up my phone and sent him a quick text: "Hey! Had fun tonight. Did you make it home okay?"

Ten, fifteen, then twenty minutes passed in silence.

Amy and my thinking brain started rationalizing. *It's okay to text again, right? I mean, maybe it didn't go through. Maybe his ringer is off . . . but if the messages show up on his screen, he'll see them and respond. Everyone likes to know when people worry about them, right?*

I quickly grabbed my phone. "Sorry to text again, just checking to make sure you got home okay."

Another ten, fifteen, twenty minutes.

What if he got in a car accident on the way home? What if he was attacked walking into his apartment complex? What if he needs help? What if he ate some of his leftovers and choked? What if . . . ?

My poor amygdala was having a heyday, playing a Choose-Your-Own-Adventure game with an increasing array of doom scenarios.

I should call. Yes! I'll call! And I'll also Google—maybe I can find his house. If I don't hear from him, I should definitely check on him at home to make sure he's okay.

The sudden vibration of my phone startled me so much that I dropped the Blackberry onto the stone floor, eliciting a protective bark from Roscoe. I grabbed it—still ringing—but it wasn't Adam. He's definitely dead, right?

Seeing a dear friend's name on the screen, I gulped down the lump in my throat and answered, not with a greeting, but with an explosion of worry.

"He's not texting back. I'm sure he's dead. I'm Googling him so I can find his address and go make sure he's okay!"

She burst out laughing and stepped in as a proxy for my hijacked thinking brain.

"NO! Absolutely not! I don't even want to know how many times you've texted him . . . and by the way, each text likely made it less likely that he will reply. Calm down. Make some tea and snuggle your pup."

My cheeks began to burn with embarrassment and shame as I stared at the log of sent text messages. I had once again spiraled down the road of amygdala disaster stories and trauma-driven reactions. In my rational moments, I could own the behavior as "crazy"—I'd become well practiced in applying this cognition to my trauma-driven Self. Nevertheless, I was powerless to quell the emotional hijack that happened if someone I cared about didn't text or call when they said they would. In moments of perceived threat like these, Amy would pull me into a whirlwind of panic and drive her CASE for survival even more deeply into my brain, linking my experiences of real trauma with the painful aftereffects: the dark cloud of shame, the belief that I was crazy and broken.

You might ask why these aftereffects weren't enough to break this cycle of emotional angst. The answer is dopamine, the feel-good chemical that floods the brain when we experience something pleasurable (Fernando et al., 2013, Steinberg et al., 2020). But while we usually associate dopamine with experiences like eating a delicious meal or receiving a compliment, it also shows up when we avoid physical or emotional pain (Frick et al., 2022). This reward response serves as a powerful motivator, encouraging us to seek out similar experiences in the future and driving us to engage in behaviors and decisions that were previously successful. Thus, when Amy succeeds in keeping you alive, the brain rewards you with a significant burst of dopamine to reinforce the survival behavior.

In these dating disaster scenarios, my trauma reaction was driven by the belief that there was something I needed to do to rescue the other person from a fate like John's. In fact, the reaction was really about helping *me*. The brain yearns to find the escape from the trauma it has known. My brain would receive a dopamine dump every time I was reassured that the person on the other end of my panicked frenzy wasn't actually dead. If I could ensure that person was safe, or (as my illogical fear-driven brain reasoned) at least intervene before they died, I would be relieved of having failed another human the way I had failed John. Even though this was an awful lot of responsibility to carry for things beyond my control, it sure felt logical to a traumatized brain like mine. Remember, the amygdala can turn down the impact of the thinking brain in a moment of perceived threat (Méndez-Bértolo et al., 2016).

Unfortunately, the experiences connected to a CASE for trauma are not experience dependent. They expand out and can fundamentally alter our overarching CASE for the Self. My brain began to revisit some very old pathways tied to shame and a fundamental sense that something was wrong with me.

A Childhood Case Study in CASE:
"Something's wrong with me."

Growing up, I struggled with undiagnosed attention deficit hyper-activity disorder (ADHD), which meant (among other things) that school was difficult for me. This was the '80s, and while I remember regularly lining up for the school nurse to check us for scoliosis, brain functioning and mental health were not a big priority in the health programs for public schools. Initially, I was found to be a "bright and verbally precocious" youngster. But combine that precocious behavior with the impulsivity and fidgets of ADHD and place that child into the traditionally structured environments of first grade and beyond, and *voila!* You've got an identity crisis just waiting to unfold.

And let's not forget visuospatial agnosia, a condition I didn't know I had until well into my late twenties, which shows up as a cross between dyslexia and spatial incomprehension. As a result, this "bright child" was placed in the lowest reading group in Mr. Scholes' first-grade class. Even at the tender age of six, I knew how important fulfilling the labels of "smart" and "bright" were to my family. Committed to proving to everyone I still deserved those labels, I dedicated my out-of-school hours to deciphering the squiggles on the pages of my older sister's books.

One fateful afternoon found me sitting in one of the oversized armchairs in the family room, my beloved cat Custard (named after Strawberry Shortcake's cat, of course) snuggled on my lap and a copy of Frances Hodgson Burnett's *The Secret Garden* held conspicuously in front of me. Watching the clock on the mantel, I turned to the next page in the book about every thirty seconds. This elaborately staged setup was meant to demonstrate that I finally had this reading skill managed and deserved to be in the top reading group with my friends.

My sister walked past me several times with a sideways glance. Then, moving so quickly and with such force that Custard fled from my lap, she shouted for all to hear, "If you're going to pretend to know how to read, at least hold the book right, stupid!"

She grabbed the book from my hands, turned it right side up, and threw it back at me. I was horrified, and the burning heat of shame coursed through my body (*emotional affective response*), accompanied by a desperate desire to melt into the chair.

I'm sure that every child who has a sibling has been called "stupid" by their brother or sister at some point, and every child has probably called their sibling the same term. It's a solid childhood epithet, benign but forceful, safe in that it's not a four-letter word yet resounding in its impact. I imagine that this moment for my sister was no different from a million other sibling exchanges of "You're stupid!" followed quickly by "No! *You're* stupid!" until our mother eventually jumped in to mediate.

But for me, that time was different. With my parents in the kitchen and my sister's friends in the family room, who immediately began laughing, my secret had been exposed, accompanied by a label: "Stupid!" (*cognition*). The label was a resounding affirmation of a quiet fear that had been building as I struggled for weeks to grasp what seemed to come so easily to my schoolmates. My eyes filled with tears and, clutching the book to my chest, I ran for my bedroom, trying not to cry and instead choking on my own breath (*autonomic nervous system function*). My retreat drew more guffaws from my sister and the other children; their laughter and words followed me that day and for years to come.

"What's wrong with her?"

"She's pretending to read? Who does that?"

"Is she dumb?"

The irony is that *The Secret Garden* has a 4.8 reading level, making it ideally suited for my fourth-grade sister and a rather implausible feat for first-grade me. But the amygdala doesn't care about such details. What mattered was the link to my core values and my developing CASE for survival.

Years ago, I asked my sister if she remembered this moment. Nope . . . and why would she? For her, it was a trivial sibling squabble as she wandered toward the kitchen to find out when dinner would be ready. Yet for me, that moment—in particular, that word "stupid"—was a definitive confirmation of my inadequacy. It affirmed an internal wariness (*somatosensory experience*) that had been percolating inside me for months as the other children in my class surpassed my reading and math skills. This moment of encoding would haunt me for decades to come.

Our internalized CASE comes in many shapes and sizes, some positive and some negative, but all reinforced for the same reason: They keep us alive. The problem is that many of these responses are harmful to the ability to live our best lives in the present day. Every trip we take on this neural freeway reinforces these ideas and encourages the brain to prioritize them. They might have hurt, but they kept you safe (Wenzel et al., 2018).

This all sounds pretty awful. However, remember what makes it possible: the brain's ability to adapt and change. The same brain powers that can lock up the brain in survival mode following trauma are also the powers that make it possible for our brains to heal.

CHAPTER 12

The Brain Will Always Find a Way Out

"How odd that if we reject what is painful, we find only more pain, but if we embrace what is within us—if we peer fearlessly into the shadows—we stumble upon the light."

—Elizabeth Lesser

Death is a side effect of life, one that some of us have to experience more frequently than others. Personally, I've faced death more than once. My first encounter happened when, at the age of ten, I began having thoughts of wanting to end my life. My relationship with death deepened when I was raped at fifteen years old and feared that I wouldn't survive. Coming home to find my fiancé dead on the floor confronted me with the death of not only my love but also my own spirit. I have confronted death while working in hospice, in the form of a patient in the midst of a psychotic break trying to murder me, and while sitting with my Nana in her final days, telling her it's okay to let go. I have faced death through a series of health complications so severe that even my doctors occasionally exclaimed in surprise, "You're still here!" when

I walked into their offices. Along with the possibility of my body giving out on me, these health issues forced me to come to terms with the likelihood that I would never be able to practice in my field again. There were two deaths within that realization: one, that my brain would never function again such that I could hold space for a patient or be present and two, that I would never overcome the PTSD that plagued my life for five years.

Nevertheless, I survived. At the time of writing this book, I've already surpassed a cat's nine lives. If anything, I'm more like a cockroach, a creature that can survive for weeks even after being decapitated (Choi, 2007). The comparison is both a joke and a real point of pride for me.

In the trainings and seminars I lead, I share the struggles of my life and the resulting experience of PTSD from my view as a neuroscientist and psychologist. This always prompts questions from the audience:

How does someone rise up out of trauma like that, especially when it has been compounded by other accumulated traumas over the course of their life?

Is there a transformative moment that can release a trauma survivor from the lingering grip of such events?

How does someone find silver linings in these episodes of despair that empower them to keep getting up every time they are knocked to the ground?

Those silver linings can show up in a lot of ways, but one of the most crucial is through the distinctly human miracles of people, community, and connection. Remember that within the EMLI created on the night of John's death, one of the most devastating meanings my brain made of the Event was that I had been disconnected from my world, that I was now completely and utterly alone.

But in fact, I wasn't. I met Lena, my grief travel companion, and not long after John's death, I found out that he had told certain people to look after me if anything should happen to him. One of them was his sister Amelia. She was his kindred spirit, his personal favorite, from the time he was a baby. Their mother has a million stories of the two of them curled up together, reading books, making up stories, giggling. That was their thing as kids, and it extended into adulthood. I could tell when the two of them were on the phone because he would be giggling. In the year leading up to his death, no matter how bad his pain grew, his eyes always shone brighter after he spent time speaking with Amelia.

Three months after John died, I went to stay with Amelia at Canada's Vancouver Island. During the visit, she took me to a psychic. While the scientist side of me struggled with the idea of consulting the supernatural, I was profoundly desperate for anything that could help me find what I needed. Closure. Understanding. Forgiveness. The shackles of survivor guilt and internalized responsibility rode shotgun with my PTSD, holding me prisoner within their vicious grasp.

My survivor guilt stemmed from failing John, not only by failing to come home as soon as my intuition told me something was wrong but also by the time I spent caring for him as his addiction grew stronger and stronger. I faced the harsh possibility of my guilt and responsibility every morning as I woke up in a world where he no longer breathed. I tried to find solace in his statements just weeks before his death that he was going to die young—he sensed that there was something bigger happening in his biology—but my guilt fought back. Wasn't it my job to ensure his survival? To find the way to break through the addiction and get him help, just like he had helped me when we first met? There had been so many times when John had helped me fight for my life, yet he was the one who was gone . . . and what if I could have saved him? *What if . . . ?*

With no concrete answers or relief in the material world, I turned to the spiritual realm. Maybe there was something bigger than me that could ease my aching soul and give me some sort of clarity.

***

The psychic said to bring something that connected us to whomever we were trying to connect with in the spiritual realm. Accordingly, I arrive at the psychic's home clutching a childhood toy of John's, a Dopey doll from *Snow White and the Seven Dwarfs*. Amelia and I follow a sidewalk lined with cobblestone bricks up to a sweet two-story Tudor homestead, ring the bell, and are greeted with a shout: "It's open! Come up!"

I glance at Amelia, uncertain. The ache in my soul is deafening. *Do I even want to know what this person can tell me?* But Amelia is brave and swings the door open, illuminating a dark staircase ascending to a bright hallway. With a grin, she gives a sweeping "after you" gesture. I smile weakly back, begging the rising nausea in my stomach to take a back seat, and begin my journey up the creaky steps.

We find ourselves in a living room adorned with the expected spiritual and healing artifacts: crystals on the coffee table, a beaded curtain separating the room into two. An energetic woman greets us with a warm smile, observing us as we observe her space.

Then, seeing the Dopey doll cradled in my arms, she catches my gaze and asks disapprovingly, "Why didn't you bring the bear?"

I freeze. There was a bear back at home, sitting front and center on my bed. The psychic had no reason to know about the bear.

Even Amelia didn't know about the bear. In fact, Amelia had given her no information about why we were there, telling the psychic only that she had a dear friend in town who would like to do a reading.

The psychic pins me with her gaze.

"The bear?" she repeats.

Suddenly I'm nineteen years old again, bed-ridden, delirious with pain from an antibiotic-defying kidney infection. I manage a call to John to let him know the doctor's orders—that if my temperature spikes above 102 degrees, I must go to the ER immediately.

He reasonably responds, "Do you have a thermometer?"

I feebly cast my eyes around the room as it swims around me. *Do I?* Of course not; what nineteen-year-old packs a thermometer when they move into their college dorm?

"Kitten . . ." He sighs. "I'll be right there."

His last words fade out as my eyes close in dreamless, fever-induced sleep. Next thing I know, a familiar hand lands on my burning forehead, accompanied by a gentle whisper.

"Hey . . ."

I stir and open my eyes to see sweet Johnny there. A giant, fluffy, white teddy bear perches beside him.

I blink. "Wha . . . ?"

John pops a thermometer in my slack-jawed mouth. I sit up, taking in the adorable sight of my long-haired, black-clad, combat-booted, labret-pierced punk rocker cradling one of the most snuggly stuffed bears I've ever seen. Once that telltale beep rings out, he pulls the thermometer from my mouth and places the teddy bear in my lap. His golden-green eyes meet mine.

"101," he says. "High for you, but not high enough." Then, with a cheeky (and relieved) grin, "Meet Sempiternal!"

Again, I blink and shake my head groggily. "Sempi . . . ?"

"Forever, everlasting. Like us. Sempiternal. Sempi's a good name." He kisses me gently on my forehead and lays me back down on the bed, tucking in the bear beside me. "Rest. I'm always here."

He grabs a book off my shelf as I drift off, my cheek resting on Sempi's fuzzy head, my mind whispering *Forever*.

I'd considered bringing the bear but decided against it. While Sempi was a token of our relationship with each other, he was still mine, whereas Dopey was specific to John alone. Feeling stupid, I mutely hold the beloved childhood toy out to the psychic, offering a weak smile. The psychic manages a thin smile in response. My stomach turns over. There will be no forever.

We spent ninety minutes with the psychic, most of it intense and bizarre, a lot uncannily accurate. Was there closure? No. Could there have been? Again, no. Today, many years after his passing, I know that there will never be closure. Instead, there is the journey of love and loss. There is my relationship with John and with the choices he made, which were ultimately beyond my control. There is my relationship with myself, with the choices I made and had to continue making: to acknowledge the pain, to stand firm against the old survival strategies warring within me, to keep breathing despite it all.

When We Don't Want to Breathe Anymore

The issue of closure comes up in another question that people ask when I share my story of traumatic grief and PTSD, the long-standing struggle with survivor guilt, which piled atop my decades-long struggles with depression and anxiety: "How did you resist the temptation to just end it all?"

It's a good question. After all, trauma and suicide are very good friends. Remember, there's a thirtyfold increase in suicide-related risk factors for individuals who have four or more ACEs (Hughes et al., 2017); moreover, these risk factors are shown to be up to six times higher for people who have PTSD (Fox et al., 2021).

My initial answer to the question is simple: "It wasn't easy."

Though of course, in some respects, suicide *is* easy. Resisting that temptation is where the hard neurobiological work comes in.

While having suicidal thoughts can be quite scary, it's a part of being human. It's an escape hatch for the brain when life feels unbearable and change feels impossible. When the brain is exposed to stress and/or trauma, it will jump into an extremely fast electro-chemical state called *gamma wave state* (Oya et al., 2002; Sato et al., 2011). This is specifically true for individuals who, in the wake of an EMLI, feel trapped in inescapable emotional pain (Ballard et al., 2020). Suicide offers one option for removing that last letter, the I that stands for *Inescapable*, a way for the brain to remind itself, "There is a way out!"

Having the thought doesn't mean we will act on it, but it certainly can be terrifying to experience these thoughts. As a society, we are taught to approach thoughts of suicide with fear, even judgment. Those heartbreaking admonishments from survivors are usually some version of the following: *"How could they do that to the people who love them?!"* This is why those who struggle frequently tend to keep thoughts of suicide hidden. I thought and wrote about suicide many times in those three months from the time of John's death to the day I visited Amelia, but I kept those thoughts between myself, the universe, and my journal. This secrecy only deepened the experience of isolation and the feeling of shame, both of which heighten the likelihood of a suicidal thought moving into action.

Let's turn to the idea of shame for a moment. As shame expert Dr. Brené Brown (2013) defines it, shame is "the intensely painful feeling or experience of believing that we are flawed and therefore unworthy of love and belonging—something we've experienced, done, or failed to do makes us unworthy of connection." As my own trauma reactions have shown, the aftermath of a trauma experience or reaction often features deep shame and regret. That's because Amy the amygdala is a shame junky. She supports the development of shame freeways through the brain with the counterintuitive purpose of keeping us safe within our communities. The links between survivor guilt and shame are also very strong, activating a primal threat response connected to the fear of doing something so wrong, so bad, that we are removed from our village. Hence, Amy the amygdala's love affair with shame—it connects directly to her core value of being deserving of love and belonging.

I carried deep shame that after my ultimatum, after John left just one week before he died, I had put that ring back on my finger and carried on with the wedding planning. My survivor guilt plagued with me with an endless litany of *"What ifs . . ."* of different choices I could have made to save his life. Being in my brain was, in and of itself, an Inescapable experience.

Furthermore, the trauma filter in my brain continued to create more and more opportunities for shame to be entrenched into how my brain made sense of the world. Shame was a key part of the freeway that was strengthened in my brain after the disaster at the comedy show. As embarrassing as it was to bolt from the theater, it was Amy's way of protecting me from the shame of people seeing my panic and tears—or of doing something even more shameful, like jumping up onto the stage and administering CPR . . . can you imagine? My survival brain was propelling me in the opposite direction from the possibility of being shamed.

Shame's original intent is to keep us in line with the cultural norms of our community so we will not be kicked out. In the twenty-first century, the story may read a little something like this: If we meet our caregivers' "norms," then we are assured survival. But if our caregivers are living in their own CASE for survival, then the things they teach us about the requirements of the community may not meet the norms of the larger world around us. This is clearly illustrated by my family's maxim that we should always be "fine." In other words, our survival norms can be perverted from the beginning.

***

I'm eleven years old and I'm frantic. We've just returned from a road trip with family and friends, my bully included, in all her vicious glory. My saving grace on the trip is a tiny notepad, the only place I can safely give voice to the deepening agony and darkness I live with.

Only now, I can't find it. Anywhere. It's gone. My stomach is clenched in fear. *What if someone sees it? What if the bully has it?* I cough and retch at this terrifying thought; dry heaving curls me over at a ninety-degree angle. Finally, the fear propels me into my parents' bedroom to inquire if they've seen it.

Shaking, I walk down the short hallway to their room and see my mom standing just inside the door, her head bent, a look of worry on her beautiful face. Hearing my tentative approach, she turns. My tiny notebook is held in her hands, open. I can see my thick black scrawl on the pages. The worry on her face feels like a sucker punch. Fear begins to percolate, then quickly turns to anger. I lunge at her at her and grab it from her startled hands.

"*NO!*" I screech. "You can't read it! It's for a book I'm writing. It's private!"

She reaches out to comfort me, but I step back as shame starts flooding in. I can now see the page she is reading—one that details how I pray to never wake up. How I wish I was anyone other than the disgusting and awful being that is me.

I run out the front door and race to my favorite hiding spot, a group of massive pine trees I had mastered climbing. Safely perched twenty feet above the ground, I review my writings. There is nothing in these pages that met the requirements of being "fine." I cry and pray the world will simply swallow me up.

Eventually, I return to the house. My mother, in the kitchen making dinner, offers a cautious smile followed by the strange words, "I'll take care of it."

One week later, I'm taken in for an unexpected doctor's appointment that would begin my journey to be free of cystic acne through the use of Accutane. The journal won't be mentioned again until ten years later, when I'm in residential treatment for an eating disorder. During a family therapy session, I finally muster up the courage to ask my mother if she remembers this experience. As her eyes well with tears and she takes my hands in hers, she tells me, "Of course. It broke my heart. I hadn't realized how much I had failed you. And when you went to climb your tree . . ."

She knew about the tree? I'm stunned.

". . . I knew you wouldn't talk to me. I did everything I could to fix it. I tried to make the bully stop and also make it so you couldn't be teased about your physical appearance." She wraps me in a gentle hug and says quietly into my hair, "I didn't do the right thing. You needed real help and you needed your mom. I'm so sorry."

I'm lucky that, as adults, we could sit and cry together about the ways her own complicated life journey inevitably intermingled with mine. She did her best within her own CASE for survival. She loved me the best way she knew how.

***

What happens when we discover that everything we thought we knew about how to stay safe, lovable, and successful turns out to be wrong? Those perverted norms that keep us safe-ish in childhood are so deeply connected into the Self that any attempt at assimilation can feel impossible. In a traumatized brain, shame takes on a life of its own, existing outside its evolutionary purpose. Add in the development pressure that whispers, *Shouldn't you have already figured this out?* and our brains may easily begin to experience our thoughts and behaviors as being abnormal, broken, crazy. As these beliefs compound on each other, it can become easier for the brain to see suicide as the only escape.

When someone is in the midst of a suicidal crisis, the amygdala is reaching its last resort for escaping the pain of not being safe, not being loved nor belonging, and not having any hope for success. This is why it does no good to ask someone in that crisis state to think about their how their loved ones are going to feel—their thinking brain is not available to them. Amy is at the wheel, and all that matters to her is finding a way out of pain.

A brain in suicidal crisis shares many traits with a brain that has experienced trauma. Both are:

- Feeling scared, because even having suicidal thoughts (or trauma reactions) is scary
- Feeling isolated, engulfed by a deep sense of being alone in the world
- Experiencing a decrease in impulse control and impaired decision-making processes
- Racked by a sense of desperation and possible urgency
- Suffering from a decreased sense of connection with and trust in humanity

Ultimately, what puts people at the most risk of suicide is the trifecta of anxiety/panic, agitation, and insomnia. That third factor is critically important. If we're not sleeping, there is no break from the pain and no chance for the brain or body to recover from the compounding effects of stress. This makes us even more reactive and vulnerable to increasing agitation and panic.

I lived in this nasty cycle off and on for a long time after John's death. Sleep brought either dreams of him, only for me to wake and find him gone, or else nightmares that rehearsed all the bad things I'd experienced across the course of my life. It was as though the protective coverings my brain had wrapped around all my earlier trauma were also set aflame. The brain has a limit on the burdens it can carry, and for me, John's death was the straw that broke my amygdala's back. And thoughts of suicide had long been a comforting escape route for my brain, making it a very easy go-to when living in my head felt too painful.

No one knew how deep the darkness truly had become within me. But I suppose some part of me also knew that I had come too damn far to let the darkness win.

***

After our time with the psychic, Amelia drives us to a lake in the mountains on the northern end of the island. Our quiet conversation matches the rolling fog that has covered up the formerly sunny skies. We had planned to go swimming, but with the day having suddenly cooled, we're unsure of our purpose now.

The beach is a far cry from the comfortable sandy beaches I left behind in Los Angeles. Nevertheless, it is beautiful—covered in stones, with a massive fallen tree trunk extending across the water from an adjacent shore. The cloud cover thins to reveal just the ghost of the sun shining through. To me, it offers a powerful parallel to my own light I was seeking within. *A ghost, a glimmer, is all that I need.* The fog settles over the trees, enveloping them in mystery. *Where do I go from here? What will come next?*

For a moment, Amelia and I hold each other's gaze. An unconscious understanding of what must be done passes between us. We exit the car, silently strip to our bathing suits, and begin wading into the icy mountain waters. Our shocked gasps quickly give way to giggles, then to a deep, muffled, mutual sob.

This is life now, I think. Spirited moments of engagement lost to the agonizing reminder. *He's gone.* Suddenly, this moment takes on a new significance for me. It becomes a moment of do or die. How does one keep breathing after something like this happens?

The answer is to dive in.

The water is ice cold. Ducking beneath the surface, we begin to swim. It is almost as though our souls have formed a pact that if we can swim to the tree, we can get through this.

As it is with water, it is with life: The more we move, the more possible it becomes. Sure enough, as our arms and legs struggle against the frigid water, the cold ceases to be shocking and starts feeling like opportunity. *We're going to figure it out. We're going to live what he knew was possible, even though he will not be there to share it with us in body.*

The fog shifts, opening to the hazy sun. A lone owl hoots its soulful tune. We feel John with us, and it is electric.

And we reach that beautiful tree, once so intimidatingly far away.

Then we float, stranded between the pain of the past and the uncertainty of the future. Finding solace in the present moment.

This is the moment when suicide stops being an option for me. This is when I start to feel Johnny walking with me, sometimes carrying me. His wings lifting my burden. His spirit protecting me.

CHAPTER 13

Phoenix Up!

"We adapt to adversity by orienting to our strengths,
attending to our pain, and taking charge of
the narrative that defines our lives."

—Arielle Schwartz

The haunting question of "why" continued to linger in my mind like an unsolved riddle. *What is the meaning in this?* I was still lost in a world tainted with grief and anguish. The inability to wake up from this surreal nightmare plagued my soul. How could this be my life? The concept of life itself felt foreign and uncertain. Why did John have to go (or, as I thought of it in darker moments, "*get to go*") while I was left behind? How was I going to build a new life when my brain seemed committed to fighting me with every breath? As I grappled with profound uncertainties and the ongoing onslaught of trauma symptoms, the persistent search to find meaning in his death weighed heavily on me. The meaning did reveal itself, though not in the illuminating burst of clarity I longed for. Rather, the "why" came in the same way as the "what." Just as every moment in our lives is created by all the moments that came before, the meaning within tragedy, trauma, and grief is created by the meaning we've found in other parts of our lives—the joyful, the uncertain, the mundane. To this day, even in the process of writing this book, I continue to see new levels of the meaning behind my experience.

Resilience builds in us in the same way: bit by bit over the course of our lives, whether we are aware of it or not. There's no once-and-for-all moment where we discover our wings and rise from the ashes. The story of the phoenix, after all, is one of cyclical destruction and regeneration. Every descent into the flames ushers in a new season of life and peace, a peace that includes the expectation of another descent, another renewal. The cycle itself is the promise we can reach for within our darkest moments. The opportunity to release ourselves from darkness lies in remembering the places where there was light.

My First Phoenix Flight

In 2001, I was diagnosed with a serious cardiac arrhythmia, a side effect from over ten years of battling against my body. My eating disorder had been driven by my amygdala's deeply rooted belief that as long as I looked a certain way, I would be safe. Now, on the heels of a life-threatening diagnosis, Amy had proof of how wrong that belief had been. I took a leave of absence from school and admitted myself into a residential treatment program. The program was critical in reformatting my relationship with food and my body, but my real treatment began when I came home and started to understand that there were other possibilities for my life and my sense of worth. When I came out of treatment, my eating disorder was in remission, but the pain that drove me was still ever-present. I quickly realized that until I started to live for me rather than others, I would never find peace within my ravaged mind.

I committed myself to the betterment of humanity because it helped me feel like I had a purpose. I quit my job in logistics, stopped modeling, began volunteering, and eventually began working for the Center for Autism and Related Disorders. John was with me every step of the way, walking with me, exploring with me. Upon leaving the hospital, I embarked upon another bachelor's degree, this time in psychology. I had amazing professors in my program; two in particular—Dr. Thomas White in philosophy and Dr. Michael Foy in psychology—shone their lights upon me and inspired me through their belief in my capacity.

Dr. White helped me understand the depths of the human psyche in ways that I had never recognized before. His mentorship gave me courage to assert my independence from the cultural norms around me. I remember the day I walked into Dr. White's philosophy class with my head shaved, my way of embracing what I'd been learning from him: that different is an exciting possibility.

He winked at me and said, "Cool 'do, dude."

I bravely responded, "It *is* cool." It was.

With Dr. Foy, a psychophysiologist, psychologist, and neuroscientist, I began to grasp the incredible peace that comes when we look at human foibles through the lens of the brain landscape and information-processing experiences. When we pull back the curtain on emotional engagement, betrayals become objective rather than personal, and human flaws become understandable rather than shameful.

It was while studying conditioned taste aversion paradigms* in the depths of a rat lab that I finally discovered the capacity to separate

---

* Conditioned taste aversion is a learned association between a specific taste or food and a negative consequence, resulting in a subsequent avoidance of that taste or food. This paradigm is often used in research to illuminate fear and learning processes.

my Self from what my brain was doing at any given time. At that point, my brain was still constantly wanting to harm me; decades of learned behavior do not dissipate overnight. But seeing how the rats' avoidant behaviors mirrored mine showed me that fear is taught and thus does not have to define us. Slowly, I developed an understanding that my intentions and personal agency may not line up with the choices that my mammalian survival brain were making to keep me safe. In other words, I began to see that my brain's desire to hurt me was not my own conscious choice.

Nobody had ever told me that Self can be one thing and the brain another. Nobody ever explained to me that the amygdala will frequently work against us in order to "help" us, that survive and thrive did not always work in concert. I started to figure that out through hours and hours of intense study and philosophical conversations with John. He seemed to understand the nature of humanity implicitly, and he was a powerful guide into exploring my internal world.

I'll never forget when the impact of the separation between the "brain" and the "Self" first clicked for me. Like a toddler awakening to the fact that the person staring back from the mirror is in fact herself, I looked at my world and, for the first time, introspected with a deep curiosity rather than with shame and self-loathing. *Why have I been hurting my body? Why am I so vicious in my thoughts about myself? How does it make sense to hurt myself in the name of survival?*

Lead with curiosity, and the world changes. In that first moment of objective introspection, I foundationally changed my ability to make sense of the complicated relationship between my sense of Self, my deservingness, and my body.

In the early 2000s, I engaged extensively in traditional psychotherapy. While it helped, psychology at that time didn't have the data we have now about how to help people transcend painful moments and have these incredible healing insights, all in just moments. It took years of challenging my thoughts, introspecting, and drawing tenuous links between the pain and the survival drive for my internal curiosity to finally spark my desire to live.

Ten years later, I was again at a phoenix moment in my life. Since that devastating day in Therapist X's office, my mind and body had toyed with ideas of suicide as a way out of the pain. In that moment at the lake with Amelia, though, my mindset changed. The trauma still resonated. I still didn't know how to go forward. But from that point, I came to understand a vital and sustaining philosophical truth: If we are fully alive before death takes us, then we will be fully alive after. What death takes from us is the ability to interact physically with those we love. Nevertheless, our essence lives on.

Before loss, let there be life. After loss, life will live on.

With each breath, I recommitted to living and fulfilling the dreams John and I had created together.

CHAPTER 14

Momentum Comes Crashing Down

"The secret of life, though, is to fall seven
times and to get up eight times."

—Paulo Coelho

March 30, 2010, is a beautiful, expansive, blue-sky day, the sun shining brightly at 8 a.m. I'm driving to work with the windows down, the wind flowing around me. There had been no nightmares the night before; I woke with a light spirit. Feeling inspired, I loaded my playlist with inspiring music, and Cloud Cult, one of my favorite bands, blasts my self-proclaimed anthem through my car stereo: "No One Ever Said It Would Be Easy."

You're a pretty human being.
Yeah, you're a pretty human being.
When it all comes crashing down,
try to understand your meaning.
No one said it would be easy.
This living, it ain't easy.

It's almost exactly five months since my Nana died, nine and a half months since John died. This living ain't easy, but it's doable. I know I am lucky—I'm going to work at a clinic with people I love, doing work that is deeply meaningful to me in a place where I feel like I have a family in my recovery journey. The sun is shining, the air is crisp, the song is right. On this day, life feels possible. My phoenix is starting to rise again.

I stop for the red light at San Bernardino Avenue, tapping my fingers on the steering wheel, singing along.

> And everything you need is here,
> everything you fear is here,
> And it's holding you up.
> It just keeps holding you up.

The last stanza always hits me deep. My throat tightens, and I struggle to not let the tears fall. Today, though, these are not tears of sadness but of the recognition of the power of the human spirit and its larger connection to the world. Even when we are weak, others will arrive to carry us through. I think of Lena and smile. Everything we need is here, when we welcome it.

The light changes and I ease forward into the intersection, preparing to turn left.

Suddenly Amy is front and center: *Something is wrong.*

A Ford Expedition is screaming down on top of me. Not braking. This is one of those surreal human moments when time slows to a crawl. My brain is taking in data in microseconds. I see the driver. She's older, maybe in her sixties. Close cropped brunette hair. Not looking at me. Not looking at the road. In fact, she's holding her phone in front of her face.

No. No. No. NO!

I'm rapidly calculating my options, which are in fact none. I lay on the horn as hard as possible. In slow motion, she looks up.

Then I see stars. I am spinning. I feel my head snap back and then forward again. From somewhere deep within me, a disembodied voice whispers, *Coup contrecoup—that's not good.*[*]

The car and I keep spinning until we lurch to a stop, so quickly that I feel it teeter on two wheels for the tiniest moment. I realize that my foot must have been pumping the brake the whole time.

Pump the brakes. Turn into the skid. Go with it until you can take control. Bodies hold *procedural memories*, wonderful things that can be encoded as early as just a few months out of the womb, sometimes even in utero. These memories are the reason we can still ride a bike after not being on one for five, ten, or even fifteen years. My body has flashed back to a memory encoded all the way back in 1995, in a moment of losing control of my car on black ice. Spinning wildly, like I am right now, I had to make the terrifying split-second choice between crashing into rushing traffic or careening toward a lake, my only prayer that I could hit a tiny fire hydrant on the side of the road and avoid being swallowed by the icy cold water.

I was incredibly lucky and did manage to hit the hydrant— *hurrah!*—but in the process, I decimated my car's axle. With the steering wheel bent at a ninety-degree angle, my car and I limped our way back up the street to my house. Of course, as soon as I exited the vehicle, my feet promptly took flight on the ice, leaving me flat on my back, wind knocked out, waffling between tears and laughter.

---

[*] A contrecoup brain injury is a common experience in car accidents wherein the brain is sustaining cerebral bruising (Payne et al., 2023).

Enter Mr. Gary Truitt, proud son of a military family. His father, my amazing Boppie, flew Navy jets during WWII; when the Vietnam War began, Dad joined the Army Rangers; Mr. Gary Truitt does not do things halfway. It's not about the war, he used to say, it's about service to the country.

In short, my dad was (and is) larger than life. At fifteen years old, telling him that I had done something so stupid as losing control of my car and diverting it into a fire hydrant was terrifying.

To my surprise, he was calm and cool. Even teased me about it. Isn't it amazing how we create personas around people? Ah, but lest he fool me. That weekend, he followed me and my sad sideways car to the auto repair shop to get the broken axle fixed. Riding shotgun on the way home, he began to grill me about driving protocols. My brain started sending off alerts. *Oh no, here it comes. Please answer correctly, Katy, so the grilling stops!*

But I underestimated Mr. Gary Truitt. A few questions into our conversation, just as I was patting myself on the back as an amicable silence seem to rise between us, the eyes beneath his furrowed brow slowly zeroed in on his target: a patch of black ice on the road in front of us. The next thing I knew, we were flying through space, gliding weightlessly across the blacktop. As my stunned glance met his sly grin, he calmly inquired, "So what do I do?"

Don't panic! Don't panic!

Under his calm gaze, my panic calmed, and I remembered what he had taught me.

Turn into the skid and pump the brakes. Don't fight the speed; lean in to the skid. Go with it. Create slow pauses until balance comes back and you're in control.

If only my fifteen-year-old brain had been able to extrapolate the gift he was giving me in that moment: a life lesson in learning to lean in. Still, thanks to that fateful lesson, my twenty-nine-year-old brain knows to lean into the skid and pump the brakes.

When it all comes crashing down, no one said it would be easy.

I'm staring at that expansive blue sky, frozen in physical and emotional shock. *Where did it go? How did that moment of possibility get ripped away?*

Then I do the thing you're not supposed to do: I jump out of my car. I know I'm injured, but my mind doesn't care. I see the other driver, smoke rising from her hood. She's not moving and I'm worried. Norepinephrine is a powerful brain chemical; it will numb our own physical injuries in the interest of saving another. In *Tribe*, an insightful book on the human social psyche, author Sebastian Junger (2016, p. 55) explains, "Humans are so strongly wired to help one another—and enjoy such enormous social benefits from doing so—that people regularly risk their lives for complete strangers." We are biologically designed to self-sacrifice for one another in the interest of the survival of the species. But as I'm rounding the side of my own smoking car, an authoritative female voice stops me with a command.

"Get away from the car. Sit on the curb and stay still. Don't move. You're hurt. The ambulance is coming."

Some odd universal energy is on my side this morning. Or perhaps it's just my two guardian angels, Johnny and Nana, already on the scene. As it turns out, a police officer had been sitting at that same light and was an audience to the entire spectacle.

I sit on the curb. Shocked. Stunned. The pain of the whiplash and the burns from the airbags haven't yet seeped into my consciousness. My brain is fully occupied in the struggle to put a narrative together.

After ensuring the other driver is lucid and not in immediate danger, the officer approaches me and again states, in an attempt to reassure me, "The ambulance is on its way."

I look up at her, wincing as searing pain starts to break through. "I'm sorry."

The words leave my lips before I can stop them, a mantra tied to a lifetime of apologies.

She seems confused. "You didn't do anything wrong. She ran a red light and hit you. Don't worry, it will all be in my report."

I nod my acknowledgment and numbly take stock of the scene. My car is completely destroyed. The ambulances are rounding the corner. Other drivers, paused in their morning commute, stand nearby, giving their statements. More officers have arrived and are redirecting traffic. The wailing sirens draw closer.

There are no tears this time. Just an "of course." In that moment, I could not see the gift of my survival. Instead, I was saturated in the painful inevitability that seemed to plague my life. Just as I thought my phoenix was starting to rise again, it implodes.

Once the EMTs arrive, they make an interesting decision to put me and the other driver together in the same ambulance. Her husband, who had come rushing to the scene in a panic, joins us as well. So there we are in the back of an extremely crowded ambulance—me, the EMTs, and two strangers. The one of whom put us all in this situation has the man who loves her by her side, fretting over her, stroking her hair, rubbing her shoulders, telling her everything will be all right. I, meanwhile, am alone.

One of the EMTs asks me, "Do you need to call somebody?" with a glance at the engagement ring I still wear on my finger.

My mind flashes back to the night of John's death. The neighbors peering in, voyeurs to my devastation, with the red and blue lights swirling outside, the uniformed men stampeding into the house, first with medical bags, then with the gurney. I was asked the same question that night too.

Yes, I silently answer, *and no. The person I need to call is dead.*

I don't want to reach out to my parents; I can't fathom burdening them any more. I wasn't dead, so what did it matter? Instead, I quietly answer, "No, no one," and clench my hands together so tightly my ring bites into my palm.

The husband asks his wife what happened. She tearfully tells him that their daughter had texted her happy birthday, and she had turned her attention to read the text and to reply. *At which point,* I want to add, *her speeding Expedition barreled through that stoplight and pushed the reset button on my recovery.* What I don't know then is that her choice will also spin my life into an entirely new journey, one that will bring brand-new levels of pain and illness I've yet to experience, which I still bear the side effects of on a daily basis. All because she couldn't wait to check her stupid phone.

I know she knows I'm there. It's pretty unavoidable when you're lying side by side in the back of an ambulance. I'm infuriated that she doesn't apologize to me. Still, a small part of my heart goes out to her. This is her birthday, and she wanted to connect to her daughter. Perhaps she felt loved in that moment. Perhaps she and her daughter have a strained relationship, and she hadn't known if she would hear from her. And now she'll be spending her birthday in the hospital.

I should feel self-protective or angry. Instead, I just feel sorry. Sorry for her. Sorry for having been in the way of her speeding car. Sorry for myself and my abject aloneness. I have people to reach out to, but I feel no connection to them in that moment. My person is dead, and I'm not.

My neck is killing me, my head screaming with pain, my chest and arms streaked with burns from the airbag. I'm transported to the Loma Linda University Medical Center, the same hospital where I attend graduate school, literally across the street from my house. They check me out, run all the tests; they don't see a reason to hold me overnight, yet they won't let me discharge myself and walk home. I'm extremely annoyed—their unwillingness to discharge me means that I will have to burden someone else with my life's latest misadventure.

I finally call Lena. She immediately leaves work to pick me up. We build relationships never knowing the magnitude of their importance. When people know we are in need, they will reach out with their inherent desire to connect and care. We just have to allow it.

***

There are times in life where it feels like we have to fight like hell every day to keep breathing. That is where I was. What kept me fighting was my transcendent tenure at the Phoenix Clinic. Not working meant being without the amazing people there. I had promised John I would keep rising up; when life threatened to propel me back into darkness, the clinic kept offering opportunities for my own phoenix to regain flight.

My story of grief and loss had been like a cloak covering me as I walked through the halls of the clinic. After my car accident, the cloak became an armored suit. The signs of my suffering were unavoidable—the remaining burn marks, the huge neck brace I had to wear. But I was adamant, I was *fine* (those old patterns . . .). I would keep working, keep seeing my patients, keep doing what I needed to do. To give up would have resulted in that swan dive into darkness I so desperately yearned for when I was walking up to the lectern at John's funeral.

I would not give up. This was my purpose.

I could not give up. It was work or die.

CHAPTER 15

Déjà Vu

"The truth is of course that there is no journey.
We are arriving and departing all at the same time."

—David Bowie

ack in my early twenties, as I finally began to heal from the lifetime of trauma I'd already experienced, I developed a plan: I would somehow be part of the growing movement to reduce stigma around mental health and increase access to care. My commitment to this purpose began on my twenty-first birthday. This is my journal entry from that day as I celebrated at the eating disorder treatment center:

October 11th, 2001

It's my 21st birthday. I'm surrounded by powerful women and smiling faces. Some of us have tubes snaking through our noses and into our stomachs. Others' arms and legs are riddled with scars. Our bodies carry untold stories of pain and our presence in this treatment center represents the hope of something different. We have cupcakes, the terror that comes with them, but also the will to make light of the terror and, in a spirited sisterhood of recovery, to consume them as though we were "normal." Mine has a candle, which I blow with a promise to myself—a promise of a different life within this pain vessel that is my body. I look around at the people surrounding me and commit to a life where suffering doesn't have to be indelible.

Ten years later, though, I can feel that inner drive—the one that had inspired me toward survival every day since that birthday—fading away. The car accident has left me with more than just a concussion, severe neck pain, and burns. My brain appears to be slipping away into a dark fog of exhaustion and confusion. I now live with the haunting fear that I'm losing ten years of focused education on neuroscience, psychology, and psychophysiology, not to mention my experience running clinics, obtaining my MBA, and participating in research initiatives. I lost my heart when John died; now, it seems, I'm losing my identity. My selfhood knows no other definition than to achieve, to drive forward, to overcome the internal concepts of being broken and a burden. The car accident appears to be the final piece of data my brain and body needed—perhaps even a permission of sorts—to cave in.

Broken Open

In clinical practice, we often talk with patients about how a single event has the capacity to "break the amygdala" just like the proverbial straw that broke the camel's back. While PTSD has been waging a powerful war in my mind since Therapist X's blunders broke the emotional bubble, Amy's years of practice have maintained my physical dissociation from pain, allowing my body to function more or less normally. The car accident, however, proves one blow too many for Amy to withstand. Years of stress, illness, and physical trauma are now flooding in, laying waste to my body.

After the texting lady totaled my car, and what felt like my hopes of beginning my new phoenix journey, all I could do was keep saying, "I'm sorry." Sorry to the cop for being a nuisance, sorry for being in the way of the lady who hit me with her speeding car, sorry that Lena had to take time out of her day to come get me and bring me home, sorry for having to call my parents and tell them I was in the hospital, sorry for even breathing. This is because something from my past—a number of things, really—was getting in my way.

I've mentioned how growing up a sick child gave me this self-sense of being a burden on my family. The interesting thing about the development of these self-conceptualizing neural networks is that they don't have to be based in fact. They only need to exist in the mind of the child to exert their excruciating impact. Once laid down, they slowly take on a life of their own. Being a burden was part of the CASE for Self that my brain had been cultivating for decades. As a result, my brain had developed a protective mechanism of disconnecting from my body, rendering me unable to tune into the physiological data points of being unwell. My insula, that core brain area that manages the relationship between the body and the mind and also a key element in what we call "gut intuition," simply hadn't developed properly. This is a common byproduct of a brain that develops within a body experiencing trauma and/or carrying sickness and pain (Ansell et al., 2012; Smith & Pollack, 2020).

Not only could I not trust my own assessment of my pain, but I also couldn't answer questions about it, not even the simple question of whether I was in pain or not. Instead, my brain taught itself to persevere through the pain until it would inevitably manifest in such a way that it could not be ignored.

***

I'm five years old, curled in a ball in the back of my mother's car. My stomach is screaming in pain and the upcoming day full of camp activities, once so exciting, now seems impossibly long and agonizing to my five-year-old self. I'm cranky and whining, "Mommy, my stomach hurts!"

Mommy is flustered. She has a car full of kids and an even fuller day. Camp is the babysitter. I catch her glance into the rearview mirror. Trying to assess me, frustration and worry flicker around her beautiful face. Both emotions are understandable. I was frequently unwell. In hindsight, I can almost see her mind calculating—what level of sickness requires a complete redirect of her day?

At age five, I'm already learning to do my best to manage that look from her. *Could* I be okay? I look at my best friend Kira, who is grinning happily out the window, chattering with my sister. Today is pool day! I attempt to transplant their giddiness into my own body. *Yes! Pool day!*

"I'll be okay, Mommy," I say.

She breathes a sigh of relief and drops us off, her car spinning up dust as she disappears slowly down the dirt road.

Less than an hour later, it's clear I've gravely misjudged my capacity. I flee my camp group, ignoring the counselors calling me back. I make it to the porta potty, but it's too late. I'm a mess, and the mess is everywhere. My clothes, the floor, even some on the walls. I try to clean it up with paper towels, sobbing in pain and shame. Attempts to clean make it worse; I'm simply in so much pain there's very little I can do except cry and sit on the toilet seat, terrified by what inevitably would come next—someone knocking on the door and witnessing what my body has done.

Within what I'm sure was minutes—five-year-olds don't get to take off into the woods on their own—but what felt like hours to my tiny self, a counselor is at the door, gently knocking, asking if I'm okay.

I offer up a wavering "Yes, I'm fine" and am given a reprieve of about ten minutes before someone insists I open the door. The smell is horrific; I see disgust cross her face before the entire situation registers for her. Seeing my pain and tears, she quietly tells me to shut the door and stay where I am; she'll be back in a moment.

Within a few minutes, she returns with a large blanket and tells me she's going to wrap it around me so no one can see what happened. She gently informs me that the children are at the pool and no one else is nearby; will I please come out? I hobble out of the small, stinky box and expose the entirety of my body's shame to this young teen's unassuming eye. She is kind enough to hold her grimace the second time but coughs a few times. I can't blame her.

Wrapped in an old blanket, I lie on a striped vinyl lounge chair covered in camp dust and try to stop crying. This was long before cell phones, and my mom is hard to reach when she's at work. She manages residential construction sites and was frequently in the field. Today, it's impossible to reach her. Still, my relief is tinged with mortification when the camp director tells me my best friend's mom, Wendy, is coming to pick me up. *How will I get in her car? What if I get sick again?* I don't trust my body.

The camp director wraps a second blanket around me and kindly tells me to bring them back when I am feeling better. Wendy arrives, warm and gentle, taking in my situation without a flinch or a grimace. She loads me into her prized Jeep Wagoneer, spirits me back to her home and into a nice warm shower, then settles me in with a cup of 7-Up and "My Little Pony" on the TV until my mom comes.

When my mom swoops in, worry etching her face, she and Wendy quietly conference. They hug and I feel relief—my body's disgusting behavior hadn't ruined their friendship. My internal "burden" story is already building a powerful freeway through my brain, and this experience was yet another grotesque layer of that internalized truth.

The Darkness Deepens

In the weeks after the car accident, my days grow clouded by a gray exhaustion that winds itself through mind and body. Time starts to slide eerily; I lose minutes, then hours, in this haze of slowly degenerating functionality. Flashes of normalcy tantalize me with hope, only to be followed by increasing fatigue so severe that on certain days I can barely crawl out of bed to brush my teeth. A second of closing my eyes at my desk is disrupted over thirty minutes later when my office phone jangles me back into consciousness.

I speak with the clinical director of my training program, who kindly suggests that perhaps I can bring a yoga mat into my office and take naps in between patients so I can at least continue completing my internship. These cat naps offer a gentle reprieve, but I feel like I'm falling deeper and deeper into the well of darkness I've been trying so hard to avoid. This darkness is different from the debilitating depression I know so well, and even from the chronic illnesses of my early years. It feels like a tar pit sucking me down, engulfing me, making it impossible to access any possibility of energy or lightness.

Time passes, and my body weakens. I go to doctor after doctor, seeking an answer, but none are forthcoming. Meanwhile, the infections of my childhood return. My stomach rejects everything I try to consume. Pain sears my kidneys and bladder. At one point, I am tentatively diagnosed with bladder cancer by a handsome young urologist whose incredulousness was evident as he reviewed my chart and blood work.

"Women don't usually get this," he says, taking me in head to toe. "Especially not women of your age. But there are certainly irregular cells here, and all of your symptoms match, so we're going to go in and do a biopsy."

My eyes fill with tears of relief. At last, a diagnosis! A horrifying one, to be sure, but maybe now we can make a plan, take some action. I'm not unaware of the irony that a "probably cancer" diagnosis feels like hope at this point. Still, it helps to finally have a name for this fresh agony and the lonely uncertainty that comes with it.

Alas, the biopsy comes back negative. Crazy as it may sound, I feel real disappointment when I get the news that I do not have cancer. Stripped of a definitive diagnosis, I once again plummet into the inescapable unknowingness of a chronic condition without a name or a treatment plan. The loss comes with a feeling of déjà vu—I've been here before, just one year prior. Only at that time, John was the patient with the mystery disease. I know how this story goes: drugs, tests, pain, and more drugs, all while just trying to keep breathing.

Eventually I am diagnosed with interstitial cystitis, a chronic condition that feels like knives slicing up my bladder, accompanied by a constant need to urinate. It's like a nonstop kidney infection, urinary tract infection, and bladder infection combined into one. And wouldn't you know, this diagnosis still doesn't offer any reason for the incredible brain fog, the overwhelming and all-consuming exhaustion, or the severe migraines and body aches that wash over me, leaving me incapacitated. Interstitial cystitis, it seems, is only one small piece of the larger medical puzzle stealing my life from me.

They say that the universe never gives us more than we can handle. I've laughed at this adage many times; still, I've often found the universe is mindful to sprinkle in gentle reminders and nudges to keep us going. In a stroke of luck, I'm able to defend my dissertation just shy of two months after the car accident, before the severity of brain fog and exhaustion have impaired my ability to stand in front of a room of my professors and prove my merit to carry the title of "doctor." Had I waited two or three more months, I would not have been able to hold myself upright in the conference room, let alone speak to "Nesting Paradigms in Hierarchical Linear Modeling."

On June 13, 2010, exactly one year after John's death, I muster the strength to walk in my doctoral graduation ceremony—a proud moment of the phoenix rising. That morning, I reread the eulogy I wrote for his funeral, proud of rising to my own challenge.

"In celebration of this amazing man, I challenge myself and everyone here to take a look at how Johnny impacted us, made a piece of us, and to start living the life he gave his entirety to for us to have."

I am determined to keep going forward, determined to find a larger purpose to it all, even as the uncertainties mount. So do the endless doctor appointments. Neurologists, rheumatologists, endocrinologists, nephrologists, urologists, and more repeat the same refrain: "We're so sorry, but we don't have an answer for what's wrong. Your white blood cell counts are very high. Would you like something for the pain, at least?"

The pain is searing, knives cutting through me. It would be very easy to numb my world through opioids, just as John had done. But each time I'm offered pain medications, my insides shudder in fear and emotional trauma. *No. None for me.* I've always hated opioids. They leave me fuzzy, a terrifying prospect for my trauma-impacted amygdala. And on the heels of John's medical nightmare and subsequent overdose, just the thought of putting opioids in my body makes me downright nauseous. Instead, I'm prescribed infusions three times a week, plus given an endless supply of other medications to, if not treat the condition, at least stop it from getting worse. My body feels like a walking battlefield, my major organs and mental function laid waste by an invisible enemy. By August, I am slogging through the final days of my internship with a brain and body functioning at far less than half capacity.

As my condition worsens, my visits to the emergency room increase, but the answers don't.

"Yes, you definitely have a virus," they say each time. "Yes, you have an extremely high fever. There is no reason for you to be in this level of pain."

How do you tell someone who is crying, whose body can't stop shaking, that there is no reason for her pain? Apparently, you write them off as a medical anomaly or (I'm sure they suspect) a drug seeker, at least until I again refuse the scripts for pain medications. I feel as if I'm reliving John's last years. Different symptoms, different doctors, different choices, but one painful parallel: the unknowingness of it all.

An unknown threat causes greater distress and physiological impact than a threat we can identify (Hur et al., 2020). When we know what's wrong, we can endeavor to make a plan or at least prepare for what is to come. But in the absence of a plan, we ruminate and catastrophize, building bigger and scarier stories in our minds, which only worsens the experience of pain (Chaves & Brown, 1987; Petrini & Arendt-Nielsen, 2020; Quartana et al., 2009).

About six months into my illness, I'm told that the school can no longer provide health insurance for me as I'm not actively taking classes. Suddenly, I find myself with no health insurance in the middle of a dire medical crisis with no foreseeable ending. A few days later, I have my first seizure.

Imagine you're calmly sitting when, with no warning, your muscles start convulsing and your entire sensory system immediately follows suit. Suddenly you're rapidly and jaggedly pulsing back and forth. Your ears turn to tunnels, sounds reverberating in a deep throbbing bass like the thunderous sound of being in car speeding on the freeway with only one window cracked open. Your eyes shake wildly, unable to anchor on a single point. Numbness creeps across your jaw and face, leaving you unable to utter a sound.

The technical term for this type of seizure is a *focal clonic seizure.*[*] Panic attacks and flashbacks have always been a regular part of my life, but this is completely different: a complete neurological hijack. Strangely, through it all, my thoughts are clear. It is a fascinating experience to be completely conscious at the same time that my body goes completely out of my control. A quiet voice muses, "Isn't this strange?" followed by a much louder thought, "What the

---

[*] A focal clonic seizure originates in the brain and causes jerky, rhythmic movements of muscle groups in the face and extremities, and in muscles of the diaphragm and pharynx.

hell is happening?!" as my body ricochets into the wall next to me. Sitting there, convulsing against the wall, I keep thinking about Jill Bolte Taylor's TED talk "Stroke of Insight" and trying to quell my panic with the fact that she survived.

Within a few minutes, my body returns to its normal baseline of pain. I sit there breathing, trying to contend with a whole new set of terrifying possibilities. *Is this a transient ischemic attack?** *Am I going to have a stroke? Did my brain suddenly manifest epilepsy?*

As luck would have it, I'm already scheduled to see my neurologist later that morning. Unsurprisingly, she doesn't have any answers for me. Instead, the visit begins a bizarre several weeks of rapid-fire stress tests and, of course, the inevitable suspension of my driver's license. I get it—keeping seizure patients off the road keeps other people safe. But how am I going to get to my doctor's appointments? Can I even go to the doctor anymore? I didn't have insurance.

Two days later, I find a check in the mail.

Back in August 2008, an insurance salesman showed up at John's office. His agenda? Sign everybody up for life insurance. But people were busy, and most turned him down. However, John—being John—felt bad for the guy. They started chatting, went outside, got a coffee. By the end of the conversation, John had signed up.

Maybe he felt a premonition. Regardless, three weeks before our wedding, he called and asked me to remind him to cancel the life insurance when he got back to the office because he didn't need it, didn't want to spend the money on it, but kept forgetting to do it himself.

---

* A transient ischemic attack is an episode that happens when blood supply is blocked to a portion of the brain, causing stroke-like symptoms (drooping face, numbness, et cetera) that usually resolve within minutes or hours.

Guess who forgot to remind him?

By the miracle of our mutual forgetfulness, John died with a life insurance policy still active. And I am the beneficiary. I will end up using almost every single penny of that policy to save my own life. This universe of ours works in mysterious ways.

Tell Me, What Is Happening to Me?

I continue my journey from doctor to doctor to doctor. The one answer they always have is the default to medication—opioids for the pain, antibiotics for the infections, anticonvulsants for the seizures. I start to wonder if drugs are in fact their own treatment of choice for feeling helpless. Scribble something on the prescription pad, tear it off with a satisfying *rip!*, hand it over to the patient— problem solved.

I can't blame them. Too little time for too many patients must make it deeply frustrating to sit across from a pained patient and not know what to do. Everyone likes to feel helpful, especially those in the medical professions. The problem was that for both John and me, the medications they prescribed didn't just fail to help, they made things exponentially worse.

***

One day, I count my bottles of medication. Pain medications, sleep medications, neuropathy medications. Medications for my heart, for migraines, for seizures, for my bladder. Medications for muscle spasms, medications for gastrointestinal disturbance. Medications to manage the side effects of the ones that came before. It's unfathomable—how does a thirty-year-old woman with an undiagnosed condition end up with twenty-three unique medications?

More unfathomable still is the oft-repeated conversation I have with the pharmacist:

"Have you ever had this medication before?"

"No."

"Did your doctor tell you about it?"

"Yes."

"Okay."

Never once does the pharmacist offer to walk me through the interactions and contraindications of a medication. I am left to assume that all twenty-three of them are perfectly safe to take together, which is exactly what I do in my state of hopeless exhaustion. Somewhere in the back of my brain, I know that those medications have side effects that, piled on top of one another in such quantity, are likely to worsen my condition. They could even be causing new symptoms requiring—what else?—more medications. No wonder I'm a medical conundrum. By that point, who could even tell the difference between the original illness and the complications caused by my overspilling medicine cabinet?

Where was this headed?

CHAPTER 16

Mind Over Matter

"Acceptance doesn't mean resignation; it means
understanding that something is what it is and
that there's got to be a way through it."

—Michael J. Fox

A moment I'll never forget: sitting in my neurologist's office, after the onset of the seizures and what felt like a million very painful and expensive tests, when she suddenly shakes her head and grins at me like a kid in *Charlie and the Chocolate Factory* who just found a golden ticket.

"Oh! This makes sense: autoimmune encephalitis."

Her announcement is followed quickly by this unnerving piece of information: "Even if we had known what this was earlier, it wouldn't have mattered. There isn't anything we can do about the virus itself. Our goal is to mitigate the damage."

When I come back for my next appointment, she greets me with, "Hey! You're still alive!"

The reaction matches the ones from my other doctors when I tell them I have encephalitis: "Well, you know that doesn't have a positive trajectory."

177

Each visit ends with an ominous farewell—"I *hope* we see you soon"—emphasized by a wary look of doubt.

Encephalitis is a brain inflammation caused either by the brain becoming infected from something on the outside or by the immune system attacking the brain in error. Either way, it is serious stuff. It sneaks up on you, making you feel at first like you have a flu or a headache. Days or weeks after onset, the really bad stuff can start to happen: confusion, drowsiness, high temperature, the inability to speak or control movement, seizures, brain swelling (which can bring permanent brain damage, as it ultimately did for me), and altered consciousness (which can include slipping into a coma and even dying). Reported mortality rates from encephalitis can be as high as 40 percent, depending on symptom severity (Easton, 2022). The likelihood of surviving without severe brain damage is much lower.

With my body under attack by such an intense virus, it is anyone's guess whether the encephalitis or some other illness or bacteria would kill me first. If I did happen to survive, it would be equally uncertain whether I would make it out with a brain that still functioned. There I was, on the cusp of launching my career as a psychologist, faced with a real possibility that I would never be able to practice again because of what was happening in my body. What an irony: to know so much about brains yet find my own brain struggling to stay alive.

Despite it all, my body remembers to keep breathing. I recommit to my original spirit creature, the cockroach. They will survive the end of days, and dang it, I will too.

Parallel Paths—Trauma, Illness, and Pain

The amygdala builds a CASE for all things that threaten survival. Just like the CASE for trauma we explored in chapters 10 and 11, Amy also creates one around pain and illness.

Imagine that, many years ago, you accidentally stepped into a hole while out for a walk. To stop your fall, you threw your arm forward, landed on it, and broke it. Today, if you were to reflect on the pain you experienced from the break, you might feel a visceral reminder of it, like a twinge in that spot in your arm. If you were to stumble again in the future, you may be instinctively protective of that once-injured arm, even if it meant sacrificing other body parts instead. This is all Amy's work. She records the sensations tied to our past painful moments, then brings them back as reminders to keep us safe now. To this day, if I start to experience brain fog, I can almost feel my amygdala starting to freak out—*it's back!*

It's important to keep in mind that, just as our bodies and brains are designed to navigate some degree of stress, they are also designed to experience temporary pain, from the slight soreness after a really good workout to the intensity of childbirth, in order to alert us that something requires our attention. To that end, pain or illness usually starts out as an acute shift from our day-to-day functioning. A pain in the stomach. The scratchiness of a sore throat. The pang of a headache. All of these are the brain and body making us notice that something is awry.

For me, though, the initial symptoms of encephalitis were masked by the acute injuries from my car accident. The brain is good at managing acute pain—*it wasn't here before and now it is, so let's do something about it.* This is a part of the pain or illness EMLI encoding. Just like with trauma, the feeling of Inescapability plays a critical role in whether or not the amygdala will build a CASE for trauma around pain and illness symptoms.

Ideally, after some time, our systems are able to move through the pain and recover. But sometimes the pain stays. Perhaps it's tied to an ongoing illness. Perhaps the body no longer has what it needs (a strong immune system, for example) to recover. It's very similar to how the thinking brain has no ability to heal the trauma after the encoding takes place.

The longer the pain persists, the more involved Amy becomes. Over time, she will develop what I call "pain glasses." Just like the "stress glasses" we learned about in chapter 11, these glasses provide an amygdala-guided view of the world designed to prevent further pain or illness. As we've already learned, Amy can take any kind of sensory cue tied to a threat-to-survival experience and, four times faster than the blink of an eye, use that to craft a CASE that will guide us into an ever-narrower definition of what is safe. The CASE prevents us from participating in our lives as we normally would, leading us to avoid tasks or situations that might possibly result in harm (Lethem et al., 1983; Zale & Ditre, 2015) and cultivating deeper pain-related fear as more and more stimuli get recruited into the catastrophe narrative. Amy's stories can even create the onset of the symptoms we fear. It's all part of an internal dopamine-driven reward system to help us stay alive and avoid that same kind of pain in the future (Wenzel et al., 2018).

Is it weird to say that this is why I love the brain so much? There's such consistency in its efforts to keep us alive, and it has the purest of intentions. Still, it sometimes needs a little help.

Let's look at an example of this in action. If you suffer from migraine headaches, you might find it painful to look at your laptop screen when a migraine comes on. Your brain's solution? Never look at another laptop screen again and you'll be safe from that awful pain—problem solved, you're welcome! However, if a friend advised you to deal with your migraines this way, it would be clear that they were being a little extreme, not to mention ineffective. The computer screen didn't cause your migraine; it's an external stimulus, the complex content* within the pain experience. The migraine itself is the actual threatening content. But since your brain doesn't know how to fix the migraine and is desperate to help you survive the pain, it has cast the computer screen as the villain in your pain narrative.

This narrative may help your situation in the short term by making you look away from the screen. But the benefit is outweighed by its psychological cost of making the pain narrative deeper and more complex. Computer screens likely had no role in creating your migraines, but now you are avoiding them. Although this may make you feel "safer," you are now risking exposure to the most deleterious effects of avoidant hypervigilance: disuse, disability, depression, and even panic about the possibility of never living a normal life.

Sick and Tired of Being Sick and Tired

I'm getting to the point where my pain and illness are becoming all-consuming. My brain is like a game of whack-a-mole—which CASE element will pop up today? Trauma? Pain? Illness? I live each day like a Choose-Your-Own-Adventure story of fear, anxiety, and pain. What normal data point from daily life might bring about a manufactured story that sends Amy spinning out?

The anxiety isn't baseless. I've been told that death is a very real option for me, given the complicated medical journey I was already navigating before this latest diagnosis. Even if I "beat" encephalitis this time, it can come back at any time. The irony is not lost on me; since I was a child, death has been my escape route, the

---

* Remember from chapter 10 that threatening content, complex content, and contextual cues are different types of encoded stimuli that can activate your survival brain into responding and overriding your higher functions.

one way I know I could stop the pain. Now I am facing death for real . . . and it isn't as comforting as it used to be. I scribble in my journal, *"Everything in my life is trying to kill me now and for the first time, I don't want to die."* I have to finish my PhD. I have to do something with John's legacy. I have an internal commitment to keep breathing.

I relish the small moments of feeling human, like listening to my favorite band, Cloud Cult, or finding enough energy to paint for a little while. These moments remind me that I want more than to be kept alive; I need to find how to thrive. Since Western medicine seems to have brought me as far as it can, I add a traditional Chinese medicine doctor and a doctor of osteopathic medicine to my medical team. As they start weaning me off the many medications, my trajectory shifts significantly. Although my energy is still nonexistent and my brain can barely function through a conversation, glimmers of possibility begin to arise. After a close friend shares some research around the role of gluten sensitivity in brain functioning, cognitive fogginess, and seizures, I cut out gluten and additional symptoms are gradually alleviated. A series of EMDR therapy sessions creates enough mental and emotional space for me to feel safe working again. My internship program remains incredibly kind and gracious, allowing me to modify how I fulfill the last couple of requirements. On a really good day, I manage to put in about three or four hours on research and report writing. I can concentrate for about twenty minutes before my brain shuts down; at that point, I rest my head on the desk and wait for the pain and exhaustion to pass. Despite the daily aftermath of severe brain fog and migraines, where I dance the line of having another seizure, I keep moving forward, keep leaning on the kind people in my world, keep breathing. My emotions remain volatile from the

PTSD, my brain still on fire with the CASE of physical, psychological, and emotional trauma. To put it succinctly, I am a hot mess. But I have committed to survival. Moreover, thanks to these people and their care, the foundation for my new CASE for resilience and thriving is being built before I'm even aware of it.

On March 18, 2011, the day that would have been the eleven-year anniversary of my first date with John, I was awarded my PhD. The significance was not lost to me. My angel was always by my side. His life insurance money made sure I got the health care I needed. Maybe it was his wings at my back moving me forward, saying, "You—we—will get this done."

CHAPTER 17

Building the CASE for Resilience and Thriving

"There is nothing either good or bad, but thinking makes it so."

—William Shakespeare

One of the reasons I could hold on through the dark moments of my journey are the signs I felt from John. From deep inside my grief and loss, I found comfort in the notion that he was there, looking after me, urging me to keep breathing. But he had help in this endeavor. His people. My people. Some I knew already, like my colleagues at the Phoenix Clinic, real-life angels who were dedicated to making positive change in the human condition. Some were angels I had yet to meet, like the man who would become my husband.

At the time of writing this book, I'm married—deeply, blessedly, happily—to a man who honors every step of my narrative, including the guardian angel who helped lay the groundwork for who I am today. The year 2023 is our seven-year wedding anniversary, a source of secret delight for me: Our lucky number 7 coincides with John's personal lucky number 23. This is also the year I'll reach age 42, a number that anyone familiar with the work of sci-fi writer Douglas Adams will recognize as "the meaning of life." My inner geek promises me that this is going to be a magical year.

I've just flown home from New York City after a series of speaking events. It's already been a full year, with hectic schedules and lots of travel, but on March 19—the date my current husband Naz chose for our wedding—we find a quiet evening to connect and celebrate us. With candlelight flickering around us, he places two small black jewelry boxes in front of me.

"Two, huh?" I grin cheekily in response.

He smiles back and we clink our glasses. Then I open the first box to find a beautiful sparkling solitaire diamond necklace. I glance at him, uncertain, surprised. I know this diamond—it's the one from the engagement ring John gave me.

"Babe?" I ask, an emotional inquiry as words fail me.

He smiles at me lovingly. "He's protecting you always. You should wear it."

I reach for the next box and, upon opening it, find another stunning necklace. The simple gold paperclip chain ends in a circular pendant studded with small diamonds, the same ones that were originally intended for the wedding band John gave me. I designed this necklace myself a few years back, but never had it made. The reference to Sempiternal, the use of my first "wedding diamonds" . . . it felt like too much freight from my past to bring into my relationship with Naz. Yet here it is in my hands, its beauty and significance expanded in a way I could never have imagined. I can do nothing other than smile through my tears at this amazing man who now walks alongside me. Who gives their partner a gift like this? Someone not at all threatened by a past great love. Someone who embraces me in my entirety. John had said I would find another great love, and that he would let me know when I found him. Now I have. And he did.

The journey to this new love was far from easy. It took grit, determination, and perseverance. As we have explored, Amy's core values are directly linked to our relationship with our community at large, but they also determine much about how (or whether) we interact with people one-on-one. In the years after John's death, I was a relationship mess. One thing I know for sure since then: Love after trauma doesn't happen by some sort of magic. To find it, I first had to deal with a very devoted, experienced bodyguard riding shotgun deep in my brain.

Meet Peri: Your Personal Security Goon

A significant determinant of our interactions with other people originates deep in the brainstem—specifically, in the periaqueductal gray matter of our brains. This part of the brain plays an important role in our general sense of safety by responding to subliminal cues of possible threats (Brandão & Lovick, 2019; Terpou et al., 2019). It also plays a guiding force in our felt sense of safety in relationships with other humans (Harricharan et al., 2016; Kikuchi et al., 2018).

As you've seen, I like to personify the brain parts that can create such chaos in our day-to-day lives. Externalizing them helps us talk about them more easily and creates space between "Self" and "brain." So, from here on out, the periaqueductal gray will be lovingly referred to as Amy's dear friend "Peri."

Reflect back to a time you've seen a celebrity on TV, flanked by a giant man in a black suit with a walkie-talkie embedded in his ear. That's the role Peri plays in the brain. The suited security guy will step between the famous person and their rambunctious fans, perhaps creating a barrier with his strong arms so the celebrity can safely pass from the limousine to the event space. And when the brain is functioning in a state of hypervigilance or fear, Peri is doing the same thing—keeping a wary watch and sometimes creating a great deal of space between you and threat stimuli, including other humans, ensuring that no one can get close enough to cause harm. Peri becomes hyperactivated in moments of anxiety, especially those involving social appraisal or engagement with other people. Peri is also specifically implicated in our defensive responses, whether these be hyperactive fight or flight, or more dissociative behaviors like autonomic blunting and numbing (Mokhtar & Singh, 2022).

My own Peri was constantly on guard throughout my life, looking out for me. The crippling social anxiety that haunted me until my mid-twenties was Peri's way of shielding me from those who would hypothetically do me harm through the sheer act of giving me love. And despite the safe place John helped create that opened my heart to love, Peri almost sabotaged my possibility of finding a new forever.

Interestingly (and devastatingly), research examining functional magnetic resonance in people with PTSD highlights Peri hyperactivation even when they are at rest. What this means is people with PTSD are likely to find themselves on edge and feeling unsafe in relationships with other people all the time, not just when Amy is acting upon encoded information from an EMLI. And Peri doesn't just get involved when someone has PTSD. He is front and center in the brain's fear narrative, working hard to keep us safe all the time, not just in moments of real threat (Harricharan et al., 2016) but any time we experience anxiety, social anxiety, panic, and more. Bottom line, Peri is invested just as deeply as Amy in carrying out the CASE for survival.

For people who grow up in an environment of neglect or abuse, as well as those with a high number of ACEs, Peri fosters constant nervousness and/or vigilance. As a result, these people have a hard time feeling safe when receiving comfort or warmth from others. This is what's behind that deep sense of being alone, even when you're surrounded by people who love you. I knew this feeling well. Perhaps you do too.

We know that before Amy goes into fight, flight, or freeze, she will try to find a *safe other*—a person we know cares about us and will protect us. When Peri is gooning for the brain, there is no experience of a possible safe other because an activated Peri sees all people as dangerous. This is why people with childhood trauma may not only be inherently nervous and wary when faced with the possibility of connection, intimacy, and love, but may actually withdraw and shut down. All things that I experienced firsthand until John's loving patience helped me navigate through them.

In the years following John's death, I had slowly resigned myself to the fact that marriage was no longer in my life trajectory. As I described back in chapter 11, I had attempted to date with rather disastrous results. My fears of death, abandonment, responsibility, and betrayal, and my intense difficulties with trust, were walls that Amy and Peri had constructed and reinforced to keep me safe. Their plan was loving and simple: *Connection caused us pain before, so if we don't risk connection anymore, there will be no more pain.*

In early 2013, I tried one last time to find love. A brief and ultimately failed romantic relationship (with a lovely man who was a vital part of my growth journey) highlighted for me the heartbreaking reality that my own trauma could cause pain for others. Realizing that, I surrendered to a future of just Peri, Amy, and me.

Old Patterns Die Hard, But
Sometimes They Bring Wisdom

The pain starts on a Saturday. A deep ache in my side, throbbing but not necessarily concerning. I have plans to go out with friends I haven't seen in a while. Dinner, perhaps some dancing. Not the best activities for a body in pain, I admit, but as we know, being in pain is not a new experience for me. I am not about to let something so trifling as everyday chronic pain stop me from living the life I've fought so hard for.

The morning after, though, the pain is a little worse. By Sunday afternoon, I feel nauseous and am even periodically throwing up. *Strange,* I think, but again, I am used to my body acting strangely. I haven't eaten much because of the nausea and so the vomit is pure bile, bright green. *Fascinating,* I think, then move on. I spend the day reading and working on articles, preparing for a full week back at the hospital. I've finally recovered enough from the encephalitis to begin a new position, and I am grateful to once again contribute to a field I love so much.

I have difficulty sleeping; I can't seem to get comfortable. As I toss and turn, the pain sharpens. I take some Pamprin and chalk it up to perhaps an unusual menstrual cycle or maybe even food poisoning. The next morning, I arrive at work at 6:15 a.m., even as the pain worsens. There are times throughout the day when I feel like I can't quite stand upright. Nevertheless, my patient care takes priority—I am still living in a state of deep disconnect, numb from most everyday experiences, the occasional flash of trauma breaking through with a vibrant flare of anxiety, panic, or fear. Compared to that, a pain in my side certainly isn't worth much time or attention.

Except for this night. With the pain increasing, I end up canceling my plans. I try to sleep but am up all night. Eventually, I call one of my girlfriends whose mother happens to be a nurse. Her mother sends back a frenzied text: *"Hospital. Now! Appendicitis."*

I blink. If this is appendicitis, I should have been dead several days ago. There's no way . . . right? Still, the pain is there, and it is getting worse. I call my doctor to see if I can get in for an urgent appointment, but there isn't any availability until Thursday. There is no way I am going to wait that long, especially given the possibility—*still . . . no way!*—of appendicitis. I look up local hospitals and jump in the car.

Somewhere along the 210 freeway, my brain and my body finally start to synchronize around the fact that something is very wrong. The pain worsens, the nausea becomes overwhelming; I pull over to vomit as cars flash by at seventy-five miles per hour, inches away from my head. After a drive that feels like hours, I pull into the emergency room parking lot and stumble into the waiting room with my body bent at a ninety-degree angle. I plead with myself not to vomit again but, before I can even check myself in, I look at the nurse and ask if she has a bag. Apparently, this is not uncommon for her; without missing a beat, she reaches underneath her desk, withdraws one, and hands it to me. Another batch of bile exits my body as I attempt to complete the paperwork.

"Are you having difficulty breathing?" she asks me. "Heart pain?"

I look at her and point to my side. "This has been going on since Saturday."

An expression of alarm crosses her face. "Saturday? Stay here."

I watch as she jumps to her feet and literally runs into the main emergency room clinical space. In a moment, she's back with another nurse and a wheelchair. I overhear her saying, "It sounds like appendicitis. But she says it's been going on since Saturday. She can barely stand up and she's vomiting."

They wheel me back to an enclosed room, the new nurse running through my vitals. "You've had this pain since Saturday?"

I nod my head.

He shakes his head. "And you're just now coming in?"

I nod again.

"We need to get some scans. Does it hurt when I push here?" He gently palpates my side and pain crashes through my body like lightning. I barely muffle a scream.

"How have you been living with this?" he asks, incredulous.

"I had work."

Barely hiding his eye roll, he mutters something under his breath I don't quite catch. It sounds suspiciously like, "Idiot girl."

A few quick scans later, I overhear the attending physician talking to one of the resident doctors. "Her appendix is gangrenous. It didn't burst; it's simply rotted away. We need to get this out as soon as possible. I can't believe she waited this long. She's lucky she's not dead."

He then walks in and tells me they have to do emergency surgery immediately. "Is there anybody you need to call?"

My mind is transported back to scene of the ambulance after my car accident, then to the night in John's apartment. How I hate this question.

Still, the doctor's words ring in my ears: *She's lucky she's not dead.* Maybe I should let my parents know. I think on that for a minute, but the messaging of a lifetime hijacks my brain with the familiar old story: *Don't be a burden.* If I die, then they will know it was serious. If I don't die, it will once again be perceived as me being overly sensitive, causing stress by my very existence. Amy's old patterns persist.

I look back to the resident. "I already told work I wouldn't be in today," I said. "I think everybody who needs to know, knows."

The next thing I remember is being asked to slowly count backward from ten in the surgery ward while Avicii's "Levels" blasts from the speakers in the ceiling. Ten, nine, eight . . .

I wake up several hours later, completely stoned from the painkillers, a bandage on my abdomen, a nurse beside me taking vitals. She keeps giving me a curious glance; finally, I inquire, "Is everything okay?" My words are a little slurred, but my anxiety is starting to rise.

"Everything's looking good, Kathryn. Is Kathryn okay? Or do you prefer Kate? You're going to need to stay here a few days. Your white blood cell count is through the roof. What happened to you is unusual. We just will need to keep an eye on you."

Her words register in a deep space of my brain. "What do you mean by unusual?"

She looks at me again and explains, "Most people would be dead. Most people would not have been able to live with the level of pain they would have been experiencing in the first twenty-four hours of your situation. This is a strange one."

I sigh. Pain has been an ever-present bedfellow for my entire life—I *should* be good at managing it by now. It turns out I'm so good, it could kill me.

She hands me my cell phone and points to a closet that holds the few belongings I brought with me. "You may want to reach out to someone and have them bring you some clean clothes."

My brain still foggy with the drugs, I first text Veronica, the friend whose mother had urged me to drive to the emergency room. She graciously brings me some clothes and moves my car out of the single-day parking lot at the hospital. The other person I reach out to is Alon (pronounced *alone*), the man I'd briefly attempted to date. I am surprised and delighted when he walks into the hospital room, accompanied by friends of his whom I had met and had grown to care about.

They visit briefly, but I have pulled them out of their weekday lives, and they have things to do.

When Alon tells me it is time for them to go, I feel my heart drop into my stomach. Tears fill my eyes—an unexpected and unusual emotional response. I feel five years old, and my next words reflect it: "But then I'll be alone."

It is as though thirty-two years of living in isolated pain is finally coming to a head. These old neural networks have brought about yet another brush with death, but this time, it's utterly and completely my fault. I've worked in hospitals, I know the symptoms of appendicitis, yet I refused to listen to the data of my body. Once again, old patterns from my past have given rise to extreme danger in my present.

I should be dead.

I am scared.

I don't want to be alone.

Alon shakes his head the tiniest bit. Then he says something so obvious yet so profound that it will alter the course of my life.

"Kate, you are only alone if you choose to be."

Choosing a New CASE

With one simple statement, Alon turned my entire life paradigm on its head.

I am only alone if I choose to be.

I have a family and friends, yet in a moment of need, I reached out to Alon, a guy I'd barely dated. I chose him because it was safe—since we were no longer dating, it wouldn't have meant much if he had rejected me. Apart from Veronica, who already knew I was in the hospital, my terrified little amygdala was scared to reach out to anybody else. What if they blew me off? Or, worse yet, told me it didn't matter? Asked why was I bothering them? I wasn't dead—it must not be a big deal.

The problem with childhood patterns is there is no choice. In those early formative years, the brain is learning to survive, sculpting neural freeways for "safety" that will become automatic patterns for how we interact with every moment in our lives, especially the moments that are difficult.

I'm an adult now, though, which means I have choice. Choice is powerful.

Alon's simple statement unlocked a decade's worth of therapeutic training. The same words and ideas I've given to my patients and encouraged them to embody, to live with as truth, are the words and ideas that my own brain has tossed aside in favor of my own fears and survival patterns. Ah-ha moments frequently work this way—an unexpected moment brings neural networks together, creating a spark of new possibility. For me, this wasn't a spark but a fireworks display. *Choice means I don't have to be alone.*

My first call is to my parents. They are appropriately horrified that I hadn't let them know I was going into emergency surgery. I then reach out to friends, who start dropping in. I end up being in and out of the hospital for almost a month while my labored body attempts to recover, but I am not alone. Because people know, they show up to help me. The final time I'm discharged, my mom comes to stay with me for a week. It's a wonderful, loving, healing opportunity that further solidifies the new relationship we began building during my time in residential treatment over twelve years ago and had been deepening since John's death. She isn't the exhausted overworked mom of my childhood nor the stressed-out and traumatized woman of my teenage years. She is strong and makes sure that I get stronger.

The old story in my brain was so powerful, but choice gives me an opportunity to write a new outcome. My new CASE is building. I am loved. I can reach out to people and they will show up. I have the power to choose my own adventure.

A New Possibility

By late 2013, I've begun building my new CASE for resilience and thriving in earnest. The idea of a romantic partner still seems far-fetched, despite the thousands of dollars I've spent on therapy trying to rewire my brain's response to romantic connection. So I turn my focus to building a new CASE with regard to my work and friendships. I get intentional about inviting people into my world—dinner parties with old friends, going on "first dates" with new friends, and building a consultation company around integrating neuroscience into trauma care.

Somehow, though, someone is able to creep through my brain's protective walls, and exploring Peri in depth helps me understand why: This man is the perfect foil for my Peri. Easygoing, charismatic, handsome, brilliant, witty, and charming, he also spends large chunks of each month traveling to New York and other international locations, rendering him safely distant and logistically unavailable for attachment.

When Naz and I first meet, we live barely ten minutes away from each other. But, luckily for my Peri at that time, I'm already in the process of selling my house and moving closer to my new offices in Newport Beach. If I have to get close to anyone, Peri is down for this laid-back, rarely home, and soon-to-be-two-hours-away-even-when-he-is-home guy.

There are other things about Naz that make him safe for both Peri and Amy. He always, *always* responds when I reach out and he keeps an open line of ongoing communication. Apparently he likes me and doesn't want to lose my interest; unbeknownst to him, his engagement and communication soothes my Amy's fear story about death over and over again. He also hates taking any medication, a critical criterion for a brain traumatized by the impacts of the use and abuse of pharmaceuticals. Little by little, Amy, Peri, Kate, and Naz cultivate trust.

Notice how the brain's primal drive for survival and safety play such a significant role in whether we allow our relationships to grow . . . or not. Even those who haven't survived intense trauma can likely relate to the difficulty of building new relationships or even trying new things as we grow older. By the time we're in our thirties or forties, we're so tied into the patterns set by our core values that stepping into the unknown can feel burdensome at best, terrifying at worst. And when the fear brain is hyperactive, it profoundly changes our overarching experiences of Self and our relationships to others. It often acts in ways unknown to us, yet its actions are always anchored in the brain's loving drive to keep us safe and safely connected to others. It's just that "safe" is entirely based on Amy's and Peri's criteria.

Just as Amy longs for security and connection to others, Peri also has another side. When Peri is acting in healthy homeostasis, one of his primary functions is attachment and connection with others. Despite his defenses, Peri very much wants to live with love. In fact, he contains a significant number of receptors for vasopressin, a hormone implicated in social behaviors related to maternal connection, intimacy, and sexual motivation. Peri is also very fond of oxytocin, another hormone directly involved in prosocial engagement, group bonding, and even orgasm (Bartels & Zeki, 2004). Much like Amy, Peri truly wants the best for us, but when our systems have encoded threat, he puts our quality of life way behind our survival.

This flip side of the Peri/Amy dynamic had come into play once before with Lena. Before I met Lena, it felt much safer, for myself and for others, for me to be alone. But with Lena, my Amy and Peri had enough reassuring information to decide that here indeed was a safe other.

Even as we start to develop safety and trust with others, Amy and Peri will still be there, assessing, checking in, doing their loving job. Even after two years together, as my relationship with Naz deepens and we begin moving toward thoughts of marriage, those fears keep resurfacing.

> *Could I ever bear the responsibility of truly loving someone else and the deep vulnerability that goes with it?*
>
> *Could I transcend the trauma of being engaged and planning a wedding that became a funeral?*
>
> *Am I even deserving of another deep love?*

Another Phoenix

On our first date, I keep the conversation conspicuously light. No talk of trauma or death. It won't be until the sixth or seventh date that I introduce that tale. As Brené Brown (2010) reminds us, "people earn the right to our stories," and the right to my story required trust and safety. Instead, on that first date, we meander our way through traditional first date fodder: work, family, dining preferences, whether we have tattoos.

At that topic, his eyes light up. "I don't have any," he says. "But if I were to get one, it would be a phoenix wrapping around my calf."

I feel my eyes get wide and try to hide my surprise with a quick sip of water.

"Why the phoenix?" I prompted, a perfect diversion from the multiple petite tattoos I've had done to commemorate my journey to Self. Again, that journey is definitely not first date fodder.

Apparently, I've asked the right question. He tells me a tale of being a Boy Scout in Mumbai, India, and growing up among bombings and riots. His pride in his young Self is tangible, enchanting, as he describes what he learned from hauling sandbags to protect buildings, carrying supplies to those in need, helping the injured to the emergency room for treatment:

"You face a problem, and you learn, and you think."

My heart warms. *Another phoenix!* That night, I shock myself by kissing him goodbye. Upon returning to my little cottage, a text message awaits me: "As you asked, safely home. Thank you for a great night. Let me know you got home safe as well."

There is no spiraling anxiety of the unknown. There is simply peace that this charming man is home and all is well in the world. I sleep well that night, Sempi and Tinkerbell snuggled in beside me. I have no idea I've been blessed with a new forever. In hindsight, I know John was smiling over us that night.

CHAPTER 18

Intractable No Longer

"The purpose of purpose is purpose."

—Dr. Steven Ruden

When interviewing family and friends for this book, I was not surprised to hear a repeated narrative of how I picked myself up, brushed myself off, and got on with my life. According to this narrative, I was incredibly resilient—as my parents called me, "one tough cookie."

> *Gary Truitt:* "She knew that when she picked herself up from John's death that she might fall down several times. She knew that, and she wasn't afraid to take the step. She just wasn't going to let it beat her. She wasn't going to let this be the determining factor of her life."

> *Kay Truitt:* "I don't know how she was able to do it. I just watched, and slowly but surely, she got better and better and stronger. She refused to give up, to quit. I really don't know how she did it. She just did."

To those on the outside looking in, I finished my dissertation, graduated, completed my third and final graduate degree, started a consulting practice, and began working toward a future that included building my own business and, eventually, working alongside an extraordinary team.

But for me, the view was very different. More than five years after John's death, I continued to suffer deeply from PTSD, activated back into trauma almost daily by what were commonplace events to others. I still lived with chronic pain and a traumatic brain injury that would show up at the most inopportune times, stealing my words from me. Resigning myself to having certain behaviors and symptoms as a part of my life forever, I closed my clinical practice, giving up the career to which I'd dedicated fifteen years of my life.

While I hadn't given up altogether on healing my brain, I had to acknowledge that I'd reached a limit. I'd tried everything I knew to do and spent tens of thousands of dollars in the process. I worked with wonderful practitioners and treatment modalities integrating psychosensory and somatic treatments along with more traditional psychotherapy. All of it helped to soften the trauma and pain, but I was still ruled by the dark journey of the previous years. The intractable memory of the night I found John still hung over me, an impermeable cloak of death and loss that my brain could not shake off. Still, I kept breathing into the possibility of some other world, life, experience. Trauma did not get to win. There had to be meaning in this.

***

In early 2014, I'm at a clinicians' retreat in Jacksonville, Florida, where I meet Bill Solz, a licensed clinical social worker. We are walking on a beach discussing trauma treatment modalities when he asks, "Have you heard of Havening?"

At my puzzled look, he begins to model what I now know as the Havening Touch®. At the time, it seems nothing short of bizarre.

"It's a new treatment modality," he shares. "It initially developed out of tapping. It's similar to EMDR but gentler and more effective. You do this . . ."

He starts stroking his arms.

". . . And you do this."

He starts stroking his face.

"And you sing 'Old MacDonald.' And through these motions, you can actually depotentiate traumatically encoded memories."

I stop mid-step—nearly stumble, to be honest—and try to muffle the mortified giggle threatening to burst forth.

"So, Bill, what you're saying is you rub your face, your hands, and your arms, and trauma goes away?"

Bill, a dyed-in-the-wool New Yorker, meets the not-so-subtly-veiled criticism in my voice with poise.

"Kate, think about it," he says. "EMDR, butterfly taps, tapping protocols, Eastern medicine and the meridians—don't they all hold similar foundational strategic components? And yet, do we actually know how or why they work?"

Duly challenged, my neuroscientist brain begins to search my vast array of accumulated knowledge about the sequencing of psychophysiological patterns of brain and body while simultaneously paging through the thousands of research articles I've read in my life. I end with a humbling void of data. Bill is right—despite the wide acceptance of these modalities by leading physicians, researchers, and organizations including the APA, the Department of Defense, and the World Health Organization, the scientific community still doesn't fully understand at a neurobiological level how or why those modalities work. How can I challenge one thing for lack of empirical data when I readily accept, and have even bet my life on, other treatment modalities that we still don't fully understand?

The continual experience of running full force into the hubris of my education is one of the gentlest yet most humbling experiences I've had in my life. It's also one of the most exciting. We don't know what we don't know. The fields of psychology and neuroscience, when taken together, are a beautiful synthesis of philosophy, exploration, and innovation. The brain is a new frontier, and my trauma survivor brain yearns to experience a new possibility. The possibility of possibilities.

At this point, in 2014, Havening is new, with only one research study thus far showing its efficacy (Thandi et al., 2015). In hindsight, that study is quite impressive, as only a handful of people in the world are trained in the modality. The hard-science skeptic in me still thinks there is no way this strange process can work. A small part of me, though—the desperate, pained Self inside of me—secretly hopes it just might.

On Bill's recommendation, I dive into Dr. Ronald Ruden's (2011) book *When the Past Is Always Present: Emotional Traumatization, Causes, and Cures*. Here is a bona fide research scientist with a PhD in organic chemistry, endeavoring to understand the very concept of what it means to be a human in pain and to find a new neurobiological way forward toward healing. It is amazing to me how much the book aligns with my own studies of information processing, trauma, and psychophysiology. As I read, the concept goes from too good to be true to something that—dare I think it?—has actual possibilities. Bill tells me about an upcoming training in New York City. To my own surprise, I find myself considering attending.

By that time, I've given up on the possibility of a life not ruled by Amy and Peri. My world will always have self-imposed rules and regulations designed to ensure the traumatic encodings in my brain don't result in mortifying social experiences. I've long since begun viewing myself as a woman who will learn to thrive *with* the devastating impacts of trauma and pain. But now, I'm confronted with something that, just maybe, could give me my brain back. With my own patients, I never foster false hope—there is nothing more painful than a "maybe" falling into a chasm of disappointment. But for me, that "maybe" is starting to brew with a scary intensity.

Creating New Possibilities

For weeks each evening, when the time comes to sign off from work, I leash up my pups and walk for miles along the California coast, serenaded by the ocean waves. Driven by the new scientific framework provided by Dr. Ronald Ruden and my own renewed deep dive into the newest research on the neurobiology of trauma, my brain has come alive with possibilities. *What if he's cracked the code on trauma reprocessing?* EMDR therapy had helped me, softening some of the trauma reactions, but the events of the night of John's death are still superglued into my brain. Both my physical and emotional realms are still regularly catapulted into the CASE for trauma and pain, hijacking my days—and life—with insomnia, flashbacks, inflammation, brain fog, and more.

In these moments, hope is like a siren's song. Stunning in its dangerous beauty, calling, tempting . . .

And then there is sweet Naz. It's lucky for me that one of his master's degrees is in computer science and artificial intelligence. My ramblings about α-amino-3-hydroxy-5-methyl-4-isoxazolepropionic acid receptors, delta waves, glutamate, and the possibilities of calcineurin only leave him slightly glassy-eyed.

Then, one night, a text message:

Naz:

I have to fly to New York that same weekend as the training you mentioned. Interested in coming with?

Me:

● ● ●

The ellipses blink as I start typing and erasing many different replies: "What? . . . No . . . Yes? . . ." What do I say? What do I do? Oh, the sneaky, singing, beautiful possibilities of hope. Then, Amy and Peri show up offering their survival-focused dialogue:

No.

Scary.

We've tried before. It didn't work.

But . . . maybe? Possibly? What if . . . I can . . . I will . . . ?

My thoughts tumble. I can feel Amy and Peri conferencing. *We. Do. Not. Like. This.* Naz's offer violates my brain's internal rules of safety . . . but what if? Panic-stricken, I finally reply:

Me:

That sounds like an interesting possibility.

I seem to have conveniently forgotten that I'm speaking to an engineer with an MBA. There isn't a lot of gray within his strategic thought processes.

Naz:

> Great! I'll use my miles and get you a plane ticket.
> Send me the info for the training and I'll find a hotel nearby.

Me:

● ● ●

My breath catches. Panic floods through me. All my internal safety signals go off at once. *NO! NO! NO! NO!*

Keep breathing. Just keep breathing, Katy.

***

It's October 24, 2014. Four hours into a jittery cross-country flight, I'm trying to watch movies but can't seem to stop shifting in my seat. My hands fidget with my copy of *When the Past Is Always Present,* its pages underlined, highlighted, and dog-eared from repeated rereading ever since I decided to attend the Havening training.

What if . . .

That hope has become haunting. Frustrating, even. I just had come to terms with the truth of my life and *now* a door has opened? I am deeply anxious about being let down and working diligently to temper the hope. The brain hates uncertainty (Grupe & Nitschke, 2013)! Cheap white wine, courtesy of Naz's drink tickets, serves to only heighten my internal state.

Remember that anxiety and excitement are basically electro-chemical twins. The defining variable is the frame that the thinking brain places around the chemical activity. So was I anxious? Or was I excited? It was hard to tell. Maybe I was both. Or maybe I was a fool. *Ugh—Amy!*

Naz gives me a grin that is an utter mismatch for my internal experience. I'm convinced he has no clue about the pressure of possibility resting on this trip. My mind whirls and spins through the past five years, my disastrous attempts at finding love, and the final conclusion of *nope, not for me*. I had given up on love. Made a conscious choice that it was no longer in the cards for me. Yet now, here is this man sitting next to me.

***

I flash back to the morning of my first date with Naz. He and I have been casually texting for several weeks but haven't met yet; building out the new business in Newport Beach means I am barely ever in Los Angeles anymore. One morning, the inevitable invitation pops up on my phone screen: "Would you like to meet up for a drink?"

As I sip my coffee and stare across the horizon, I feel my mind and body respond with a harsh *No*. But somewhere deep inside, my heart quietly whispers, *Can we wait before we reply?* Or maybe it wasn't my heart. Maybe it is something larger than me.

With a flash of anxiety followed by a sigh, I put my phone down, his text unanswered, and throw on my gym clothes to meet my trainer, Susan, for physical therapy.

Susan seems to know that something is slightly different, and she asks if I am in more pain than usual or if something has happened. Her intuition always catches me off guard—a helpful barometer for the dissociated experience I continued to live in. I take a moment to breathe and steady myself before answering.

Meanwhile, Susan moves to place a band around my shoulder and my arm. Unexpectedly, she lunges forward, her hand capturing something as it falls through the air.

"Susan?!" I exclaim. "Are you okay?"

She opens her palm. Within it rests a necklace that I had not removed from around my neck in almost ten years. John had gifted me the necklace when I started graduate school. It was our version of a promise ring; it was the promise of our forever.

Susan knows many of my stories, including the story behind this particular necklace. Moreover, she understands the mind-body-spiritual connection of healing, and that you cannot separate one from the other if true recovery is to be found. Her eyes wide, she extends her hand toward me.

"Kate! What are you doing tonight?"

Her bull's-eye intuition amazes me as much as it annoys me. It is as though she can sense my internal struggle.

"Whatever it is, you're going," she states authoritatively.

I give her a sheepish grin and grudgingly mutter, "Fine. Do you mind if I send a quick text message?"

Her eyes light up. "Absolutely! Phone incoming—yes!"

Tucking the necklace into a safe place, she picks my phone up off a nearby table and tosses it to me.

"Things don't just happen, Katy," she adds in a mothering tone. "We have to pay attention to the signs of the world around us."

John's words quietly tumble through my mind, giving me permission to lean in and take a risk. *You have to find great love again, and I'll always be with you. And when you find that person, I'll let you know.*

***

As the airplane carries me closer to New York City, I force a smile and take a gulp of my chardonnay, belatedly cursing my courage as I sneak another steadying glance at Naz. My heart flutters. Just when I'd decided to stop reaching for the moon, the moon had reached out for me. *This man. He wants forever. He wants it with me.* Still, I had barely begun walking steadily on Earth—wasn't it bold to shoot for the moon *and* the stars? My fingers tap on that same gold necklace, clasp fixed and once again resting around my neck.

Breathe, Katy. You're okay.

Breathe. Breath. Repetitive and constant, much like the study thrum of a heartbeat. These are normal things. Similarly, I remind myself that it's simply a training, just like a million I've been through before. Life will be life.

I reach over and take Naz's hand, twining my fingers through his. He beams at me; an accidental giggle escapes my lips. His adoration for me is palpable, delightful. Next thing I know, his forehead is on mine and he's staring deep into my eyes.

"It's going to be whatever it needs to be," he says quietly.

Maybe he sees more than I think.

An Unexpected Light

I'm up at 6 a.m., dressing in the darkness of the hotel room while Naz snoozes on. Sleep had not befriended me the night before; I'm groggy, but fueled with adrenaline. My thoughts and emotions have become almost combative, my energy borderline aggressive, my questions ready to launch. What I want most to ask Drs. Ron and Steve Ruden is *How dare there be hope?*

I make the bold choice to walk to the venue. I've always loved the energy of New York City. But within minutes, I'm lost. My spatial-agnostic, encephalitis-impaired, anxiety-riddled brain tumbles helplessly through the rapid-fire sensory experience that is Manhattan. My flats sting my feet and my resolve crumbles as I'm forced back into the truth of my humanity. Attempts to get my bearing require stopping to check my phone, which means being jostled by the traffic of bodies flowing around me. I'm quickly tilting into sensory overload, a very real thing for PTSD sufferers.

Our visual and auditory processing can be overwhelmed by high levels of input to the senses (Mueller-Pfeiffer et al., 2013). At one point, I stumble, and an older gentleman catches my arm, steadying me. Rather than growling at me, he smiles kindly and asks, "Where are you headed?"

I get the feeling he can sense my Midwestern roots. I show him the map on my phone, which has been chirping directions at me for twenty-five tense minutes.

"Ah, the Convene over on Park Avenue," he says, and he proceeds to give me much more reasonable directions. "When you get to the giant bronze statue, take a left and then at the Starbucks you'll go right. If you get to the church, you've gone too far . . ."

I'm sure my sigh of relief was audible. Statues, Starbucks, and churches I can navigate. I'm so relieved I want to hug him, but his crisply pressed Fifth Avenue suit indicates this may not be welcome. Hand to my heart, I thank him profusely and venture on my way, his chuckling "Good luck!" ringing in my ears. If he only knew how desperately hopeful I am for this to be a lucky day, weekend . . . life from now on? I can't even think it.

I arrive at the Convene, looking up at the looming glass doors. The drama my brain is creating is laughable even to me. A deep breath in, courage gathered, I muster my confidence and stride forward into whatever will be.

Thunk.

I run straight into the glass, my entire body crumbling into the door from the velocity with which I threw myself forward. I glance through the door and spy a lovely brunette watching my mishap from the building lobby. Catching her eye, I laugh, almost maniacally, panicky energy starting to overwhelm me. She cautiously smiles back at me and slowly advances to open the door. Gently easing it open (*Oh, it's a pull door—duh!*), her smile broadens.

"Are you here for the Havening Techniques training?"

I nod emphatically, keenly aware of the fact that I'm still gig-gling, unable to get my nerves back under control. I'm verging on a panic attack—being late, getting lost, huge throngs of people, running smack dab into a door. A familiar thought returns: *She probably thinks I'm totally crazy.*

I take a few deep breaths, then extend my hand. "I'm Dr. Kate Truitt."

I'm good at playing the part of a not-crazy, not-traumatized person. I know the gig: modulate the tone of voice, square the shoulders, make good eye contact, have a solid handshake.

"Ah! Hi! I'm Feliciana. We are just getting started, you're a couple of minutes late and so are we, so you're right on time!"

She bypasses my hand and wraps me in a warm hug. I feel my entire being stutter step at that moment, my protective friend Peri recoiling. But I return the hug.

I flash back to middle school, a long-ago memory of wandering the schoolyard deeply depressed on a bleak gray day, seeking my best friend Sara, snuggling into her. With that long-ago memory cradling me, something akin to hope begins to whisper in my head. I give my head a brief shake, demanding my attention return to the present moment.

"I'm right on time?" I repeat back, confused.

"Yes! Oh, and we have lots of gluten-free goodies for you."

She gestures to a table overflowing with treats for the training attendees. "Here's your registration information. Go take a seat!"

I'm baffled. Never in my life have I received such an efferves-cent greeting at a training. *What on earth have I signed up for?* I cautiously open a second door leading into the conference room and peer in—all things appear normal. Rows of chairs, large screens, projectors, a lectern, people quietly talking among themselves awaiting the beginning of the lecture.

I find a seat in the front row and sit, taking another steadying breath. What a way to start the day—a morning of uneasy adventure almost culminating in the all-too-familiar experience of a panic attack. Still, while I'm ambivalent about my nervous system's performance thus far, I have to note with gratitude the two interactions of kindness that quelled my panic and brought me back into a state of internal control. The possibility of hope still hums cautiously through my brain and body. When an older gentleman approaches the lectern, that hope transcends its whispering state and moves into full bloom.

Slide after slide flicks by as Dr. Ronald Ruden dives into the neuroscience of encoding moments. My brain is lulled into a pleasant buzz as he discusses the amygdala, electrochemistry, and polarized channels. As the introduction of the Havening Touch is made, I nod along. My scientific Self approves the discourse—it makes sense when we look at the theory—and my inner cynic slowly eases back. During the Q&A afterward, I toss tough questions at Dr. Ron; he navigates them seamlessly. After one particularly detailed question, I swear that he winks at me. I was not as camouflaged as I hoped; fortunately, he's unfazed by the woman in the front row who clearly needs some things proven. I'm too engaged to be self-conscious, though. My body and brain are spinning with the possibilities of the information he's shared. Could it really be true? Could this actually work?

At mid-morning, the call is made for the first practice groups to organize—we are going to try the Event Havening protocol for ourselves. I circle up with other attendees in my row, and we stare at each other with nervous expectation. The next thing I know, Dr.

Steven Ruden, co-creator of the Techniques, is pulling his chair into our group. With an affable smile, he poses a question that will change the course of my life forever.

"Does anyone have an event they would like to work on?" he asks. "Something that meets the criteria of EMLI that Ron has been describing?"

The universe does have its moments. For me, this one presented a reckoning. Innumerable hours of EMDR, somatic work, cognitive behavioral therapy, and so much more therapy, yet I still traveled the world through a haze of PTSD. What did I have to lose? More importantly, what might I gain? My hand eases upward of its own volition and my voice, previously so strong in the quest for good science during the lecture, hesitatingly stutters,

"I do."

Steve turns to me with a gentle smile. "Do you mind sharing a little bit about what you would like to work on?"

With a cautious glance around the group, I share a brief synopsis. Feeling Amy poised to move into full protective mode, I stumble through the high-level details of the story while attempting to avoid full brain hijack. I'm . . . half-successful? My physiology becomes more reactive and alert the more I share, and my stare focuses intently on my clasped hands while I try to quell the rising panic that always arrests me when I tell the story to anyone, let alone a group of people.

Suddenly, I feel a warm hand covering mine. Startled, I look up to meet Steve's gentle and concerned gaze. Within that gaze is a small sparkle, a sparkle I have since come to recognize as the knowledge of the power of Havening. He glances at my nametag. "Kate?"

I nod.

He asks softly, "Would it be okay if we began Event Havening now?"

I nod again, relieved to have someone else take charge and stop the story that brings so much pain.

We begin. As we practice the Havening Touch Bill had already shown me, Steve guides me through the initial cognitive protocol, a series of "brain games" like imagining bouncing a basketball and counting each bounce, humming a few rounds of the childhood song "Old MacDonald," counting in multiples of four, five, and six.

After what feels like a considerable amount of time, he invites me to open my eyes. (A surreptitious glance at my watch shocks me with the realization that it was only fifteen minutes.) He asks me to again reimagine the scenes that have played themselves out in my mind's eye millions of times in the past five years. I steel myself for the physical and emotional onslaught as I mentally walk through the events of that night. *Breaking open the sliding door, the mad dash to the bedroom, the dogs oddly barking and leaping around me, John's body . . . but wait.*

Something's different. There's no onslaught, no searing and agonizing pain. There's space. My brain isn't running in circles—if anything, it feels slow. Calm. So does my breath.

I hear my cynical Self jump back online with an Amy-infused thought: *This one's for posterity, Katy. Prove this doesn't work!*

I force my mind to the final scene. *The body. The inability to make him breathe. The gasping call to 911. The walk back from the gate when the truth was undeniable.* Nope. Still no pain, no panic. Just a light.

Wait. What?

I'm sure my incredulity showed on my face. Yes, the place in my memory where the body had always been is now a gentle, glowing, warm light. I feel my body relax of its own accord. Breath now abundant. *Johnny Angel.*

Even as I write this, I have the exact same visual when I return in my mind to that room. Warmth. Light. Ease. Gone is the intense pounding on the front door, so fierce it left my hands bruised for weeks; the screaming and yelling to be let in, my throat aching with the savagery of my fear; the frenzied kicking at the patio door lock; the mad dash to the back room; the bone-chilling cold and searing pain as I crashed to my knees to administer CPR; the agonizing inability to make him breathe. Instead, the memory appears to this day as it does in my journal entry from that night:

> *There are no doors blocking me. I walk easily into the home and then the room, my hand falls to Roscoe's head and I smile down at Tinkerbell. Glancing to the far-left corner of the room, I see a golden light. Welcoming, friendly. Then a warm weight settles on my left shoulder. Almost as though if I were to reach my right hand up and cover my shoulder, I would feel John's hand there, a gentle reminder of his loving presence.*

I was not anticipating this change. Even in my most powerful EMDR sessions on childhood trauma, never had my brain so quickly, so seamlessly, rearranged the traumatic stimuli of an event. Fifteen minutes! And I didn't even have to relive the memory in detail. In fact, it was the opposite. A partnership in healing with Dr. Steve through the Havening Touch and playing brain games.

It's important to note that Peri and Amy both had very strong opinions about touch. A childhood of chronic pain, constant bullying with physical violence, more than my fair share of sexual violence—it all added up to my not liking touch, except from those I knew to be safe. Yet the application of the Havening Touch was unexpectedly no different for me than the eye movements or butterfly taps of EMDR. It was a scientifically informed experience of creating a brain state that is permissive for healing.

Today, that image of warm light is one I visit for strength when my inner darkness or electric anxiety threatens to overwhelm me. But on that fateful day, the shock of this new neural memory almost doubles me over. Sitting there, a smile threatening to break across my face, I remember that thought—*For posterity!*—and diligently walk myself once again through the agonizing play-by-play of that night. Yes, the memory is still there. Nothing has been removed or wiped from my mind; I can access each devastating step. But now there is no agony in the recall. Simply that golden light, my Johnny Angel, and the weight of a warm presence riding shotgun on my left shoulder.

Well, I'll be . . . Wow.

I blink open my eyes, happy tears threatening to spill over, a grin finally breaking through. In a move hugely out of character for me at that time, I grab Steve in a huge hug.

"Thank you," I whisper, the words woefully inadequate in the face of the gift that my brain, my life, has just been given.

Then I look up to see Dr. Ron returning to the lectern. *Oh right, this is a training.* I resume my seat, trying to steady myself in the face of my entire life having just pivoted on its axis. As he begins the second presentation, I briefly flash back to my keening wail at John's funeral: *There must be meaning in this!*

My mind starts to whirl. Is this the meaning I've been waiting for?

CHAPTER 19

Walking Into a New World

"An impossibility is just a possibility you don't understand yet."

—Matt Haig

I walk out of the conference that day into a city as alive and vibrant as I feel. The energy within me seems electric. I pop in my earphones, something I haven't done for years in public (vigilance always winning out over the possibility of fun), and practically skip through those brisk and busy streets, taking in the neon lights, the shifting shadows, the warm glow of the sun as it glances off the glass buildings. This is the New York City I knew in my twenties. I stop over and over again to take photos of the scenery around me, wanting to capture this new experience so I can hold it forever in my heart. The world is expansive and full of new possibilities. My entire visual sphere has changed.

When we are living in a traumatized state, our visual processing systems are altered. We stop seeing the world as a complete, surrounding space, and the trauma filters guide the majority of our sensory processing. Colors shift and dim as the search for threatening stimuli is prioritized in our visual fields. As the saying goes, we lose the forest for the trees, except that in posttraumatic stress disorder, we lose both the forest and the trees in search of the anticipated predator—rather, in the anticipation of everything becoming a predator (Felmingham et al., 2003; Mueller-Pfeiffer et al., 2013).

But when I push open that tall glass door (the same one I slammed into just eight hours earlier), my brain is no longer scanning for any and all possibilities of threat. Instead of seeing the outside world as an elusive web of possible trauma grenades, I revel in the colorful chaos around me. The overwhelm of the bustling streets, the unwieldiness of my phone, the directions being chirped at me while I struggle to find my way—none of that seems to matter anymore. Now I can look at the map, recognize where I need to go, even listen to music as I walk. Bravely, I dare to ponder: *Is my Amy healed? Is my life mine again?*

Eventually, I notice a young man following me, something that would have formerly put me in a state of hypervigilant defensiveness. But as I pause to snap another photo, I catch him glancing in the same direction that my phone is pointed. He quickly brings out a more professional camera and catches the same photo.

I grin at him and wink (*Look at me—I'm a person who winks now?!*), and he smiles back before moving along to find his next frame. Even this brief exchange feels exhilarating. For the first time in five years, I've enjoyed an interaction with a stranger over the simple joy of the present moment.

I make it back to my hotel room and burst in, grinning from ear to ear. Naz, who would usually greet me with a hug and a grin, instead stops and looks at me as if to assess. He knows how wary I've been about the possibility of something different coming out of this training. I had all but forbidden any conversations around what could happen if everything Bill Solz told me was true.

Cautiously, he asks, "So . . . how did it go?"

All I can do is beam at him. I'm suddenly at a loss to share what happened, how different everything feels. Up until that point, the storyline he knows is the same summary I give everybody, including the group in the conference that morning: It was a week before my wedding, this happened and that happened, he was dead, I couldn't save him. And while Naz knows a little about my anxiety and depression, the panic attacks and nightmares I struggle with, he does not know the full extent of my illness or the grip of despair I've been living in. Nobody really does, aside from my therapists; it doesn't feel like something I can freely share, even with someone I might be building a future with. Thus, in that moment, all I can come back with is, "It was great! What time is dinner?"

As we eat, he shares another surprise. We are going to do that thing you do in New York City: see a show. Not just any show, but an immersive play called *Sleep No More*, a remake of Shakespeare's *Macbeth*, performed throughout five floors of a former grand hotel.

I freeze mid-bite, my hand floating in the air as that familiar ice-cold shock floods my veins. Ever since the night at the comedy show, I rarely "do" theater events like plays or concerts, and only those with little chance of activating my CASE for trauma. *Book of Mormon* or Cirque du Soleil I can handle, but a remake of Shakespeare's most murder-happy play?!

Then I remember the events of that morning. Tentative, I will my brain to return to that fateful evening in June of 2009, trying to activate Amy. Nothing happens. I stay calm, just as I did in the conference earlier that day. *You said "for posterity," Kate. Nothing could be more activating than an immersive play about murder, insanity, and suicide. This will show you how effective this Havening thing really is.* Steeled in my conviction that a research opportunity of epic scale has presented itself to me, I commit myself to the experience.

***

"Present fears are less than horrible imaginings." So goes a famous line from Shakespeare's *Macbeth*, and it rings through my head as we arrive at the McKittrick Hotel, the staging grounds for *Sleep No More*. A guide leads us through a dark maze of hallways before emerging into the Manderly Bar, the hotel's 1930s-themed lounge. Eventually, we are called upon to enter an ancient elevator. The masked lift operator hands us masks of our own and indicates that from that moment on, silence is the rule.

As the elevator begins its slow ascent, I grab Naz's hand. The crinkle of his eyes behind his mask tells me he is smiling at me. I give his hand a squeeze just as the elevator shudders to a jarring halt. The doors slide open and in front of us is a graveyard, hazy with ominous atmosphere. I check in with myself and find my breath is steady, my heartbeat a little elevated. Not with fear but, I'm astounded to note, with excitement!

The lift operator motions me out of the elevator and I gingerly step out into the fog. Suddenly, my hand slips from Naz's. I quickly turn and catch his eyes widening in shock as realization dawns on us both and the elevator doors slide closed, separating us.

I'm alone. In a graveyard.

Stunned, I look around. There are white sheets covering slabs with recognizable figures underneath. *Oh dear—bodies.* Again, I check in with myself. Breath is steady, heartbeat is more elevated, but I'm okay. I shake my head, as incredulous as I was that morning sitting across from Dr. Steven Ruden. Where on earth was my panic? Where was Amy and her CASE for trauma?

I feel as though a toxic friend has unexpectedly broken up with me, and I half want to shout into the absence of my fear to make sure she is okay, too. Instead, I stand still, looking around, assessing the environment both within my body and in the eerie scene around me.

I suddenly remember what it felt like to be a very young child: curious, unafraid, emboldened rather than intimidated by the world around me. I feel this young Self waking up, yearning to come out and play. I welcome her wholeheartedly and, alone in this bizarre setting, take off on my own crazy journey through the McKittrick Hotel.

The play is amazing, macabre, dark, moving, fascinating. There are rooms tucked into rooms with secret keys and codes. There are people everywhere wearing unusual masks, and I'm surrounded by bodies—and blood.

I skip from room to room, never knowing what strange scenes of mystery and death will be behind the next door or down the next mazelike hallway, creating my own story of freedom amid the gruesome tale. I am not fearful at all. In fact, I'm *seeking* to be activated. The play perfectly parallels the web of fear I've lived in, for five years following John's death, yes, but also for what felt like a lifetime. My adventure is to challenge the fear, to gather the evidence my scientific brain needs to believe that my brain has truly become different within a matter of hours. With each gruesome scene, hope grows stronger. *This is real. I am back.*

If we had gone to this play last night, it would have been a tale of PTSD horror for me; this was a candy store of sensory trauma cues for my amygdala. Today, I am not just surviving it; I am having fun. Present fears and horrible imaginings have no control over me now. The CASE for trauma has faded away.

Eventually I find Naz. As bloody mayhem rages around us, he cups my face in his hand and gazes intently into my eyes, relieved at my arrival but clearly concerned. I bounce up and down a few times with glee, eagerly asking, "Did you see the hidden rooms?" then pulling him along behind me. As we watch the final scene of the play—the suicide scene—I look at Naz and think, *My world is mine again*. I lean into him, and he puts his arm around me and kisses my brow.

He says, "You seem different."

I reply simply, "I am different."

Naz has never known me without trauma, never seen a version of me that didn't live in a space of stress and anxiety. I'm not the me I know, either. A new CASE for Self is growing. I'm no longer a woman fighting the demons of her past nor pushing back thoughts of needing to end it all. The future is suddenly very real, and I am excited to get to know this new me. Thanks to the universe kicking me off that elevator, I now have certainty that a whole new world awaits both of us.

The Beginning of a New Forever

Climbing into the cab after the show, I feel the pull for the one thing that consistently signifies the ending of a successful night: macaroni and cheese. Taking Naz's hand, I cheekily offer a challenge: "If you can find me gluten-free macaroni and cheese at 2 a.m. in New York City, I will be yours forever."

Oh, the audacity. Even as the words come out, I realize I am doing something I have never done in a relationship, even with John. For years, he was the purveyor of forever, sealing the deal through years of mindful and conscientious courtship. Now, on a whim, I'm the one referencing the future, the possibility of forever. Forget "I'm back"—this version of me has *never* existed.

Naz looks at me, squares his shoulders, grabs his phone.

"Challenge accepted."

I smile a secret smile, noticing that warm glowing light on my left shoulder, the same one I experienced during the Event Havening session with Dr. Ruden. I can be unstoppable if I want to be. I am the phoenix.

With a shout of triumph, Naz picks up my hand, entwining my fingers with his. With a kiss on the back of my hand, he proudly gives the cabbie rapid-fire directions toward S'MAC, a.k.a. Sarita's Macaroni & Cheese in the East Village.

As we pull up to the restaurant, he looks at me meaningfully and says, "So, forever *ever*, right?" And my heart doesn't stop with fear. I'm not paralyzed in the what ifs. I simply smile back at him and say, "Well, it's open. So yes—forever *ever*."

The moment is rudely broken when Naz notices the time. With another glance at his phone, he mutters, "Uh . . . wow— they're closing."

Our cab driver, silent up to this point, bursts out laughing. As Naz bolts from the car into the restaurant, the driver asks if he should wait. Grinning, I tap my watch and reply, "Forever depends on this man's persuasion abilities, apparently." The driver grins back at me, apparently wanting to see this romantic adventure through.

After a few minutes, Naz emerges victorious, to-go boxes of S'Mac's amazing mac and cheese in hand. As he rejoins us in the car, he beams at both the driver and me.

"Forever *ever*."

CHAPTER 20

The End and the Beginning

"Experience should teach us that it is always
the unexpected that does occur."

—Eleanor Roosevelt

I have shared before that, as a clinician and healer, I am extremely careful not to create false hope for my patients. The brain is a beautiful, complicated, incredible entity that cannot be confined to a certain number of days or treatments to see specific outcomes. You can be sure that, even though it looked that way, it did not take just fifteen minutes for my entire world to reorient itself. While I was still in shock at the extreme differences in my neurobiology after a single experience with Havening, I was a practiced-enough scientist to understand that the vestiges of trauma run deep and leave an indelible presence on the way the brain functions. The dramatic changes I was experiencing were a result of this powerful new modality joining years of careful, intentional healing work I had already put in.

***

The second morning of the conference finds me returning to those same glass doors (I remember this time to pull, not push) with a clearer brain and an anticipatory energy I have not felt in a long time. Dr. Steve Ruden greets me, inquiring how my night went and how my sleep had been—questions I am used to from my EMDR days as both a practitioner and a patient, containing subtle undertones of *How's your brain doing?* and *Did you notice anything?*

I am relieved to see him. While the internal changes feel incredible, I am also skeptical and anxious. *Will this last? And what will today hold for us, given how impactful this simple exercise of Event Havening was?*

In a manner that I will learn is characteristic of him, Dr. Steve leans in with a comforting presence and reflects to me that it might be unsettling to have such a long-term trauma experience change so suddenly. Noting that there might be some lingering elements that will need to be addressed, he says he will be happy to walk alongside me through the day as we learn the rest of the techniques.

I release a breath that I didn't realize I'd been holding. A part of me has been nervous that the work of the day before could be undone if we have to go deeper. That had happened in my past EMDR sessions—incredible gains shattered by the onset of a new memory that gripped my being and took me down a whole new rabbit hole of memories I didn't know were there.

Comforted by his wisdom—*he created this thing; he knows what he's doing*—I return to my seat in the front row, wondering what will unfold today. Glancing around the room, Dr. Ron catches my eye and offers a warm smile and a wave. Surprising myself, I freely smile back and notice my body begin to relax. It seems Peri and Amy can comfortably settle back and allow an openness to what comes next.

The lecture begins with emotions and cognitions: depression, anxiety, trauma, pain. I feel a little bit like I'm back in graduate school reviewing Psychology 101. I am impatient for the integration: *How does this come together with Havening?* I feel the hubris of my "hard-science" brain lifting its head. *Yesterday had such mind-blowing depth, and now we're doing a very cursory overview of basic psychological concepts? Where's the neuroscience? The hard data?* My inner skeptic quickly chimes in. *What if what I experienced yesterday wasn't real?*

To check myself, I gently drift back in my mind to the night of John's death. Yes, that warm presence is still there. The change in my brain is real, though I still don't understand how. I return to the lecture befuddled. *What is happening in my brain?*

Then the conversation takes a sharp turn. The previous day was focused on helping the brain release a single traumatically encoded experience through what they called *Event Havening*. Now, we begin exploring an idea called Transpirational Havening, a protocol they claim can work with the complex content and contextual elements of a traumatic encoding as well as with the CASE for trauma Amy builds. The science feels muddy at best; I can't get a grasp on their conceptualization of it. However, I know enough about the darker side of neuroplasticity (remember SISP?) that I can find my own neurobiological framework for what they are discussing.

They say they have a mechanism for addressing the neural networks that develop out of a traumatic experience. You'd better believe that caught my attention.

Is Dr. Ron really saying we can identify and intentionally focus on a neural network that has developed through encoding the sensory elements of a trauma?

That they have an intervention that can heal the CASE for trauma and survival?

No way.

I know these trauma-encoded neural networks exist. I navigate my world with them every day. I've studied them for years and worked with hundreds of patients as entrenched within those networks as I am. But an intervention that can target those networks specifically? Now that would be a revelation . . . if it were possible.

I check in with my amygdala again, returning to the room where I found Johnny, again encountering that new warm light. I then invite my mind to float forward to the experiences after I found him, the realization that I couldn't save him, the depth of aloneness as I sat surrounded by looky-loo neighbors, their quiet inquiry: "Do you need to call someone?" The black heaviness of that moment settles back in my chest. I can effortlessly recreate every sensory element: the wooden chair, the oversized round table that John had inherited from his mom, John's feet lying lifeless in the corner of my vision, the knowledge that I had to make that phone call. Anxiety begins to percolate inside of me.

Oh no . . . does this mean it didn't work?

I return to our last phone call, that sweet exchange of "I love you!" and "I love you more!" and his laughing response: "No way." My brain and body immediately flood with that awful survivor guilt, my own deafening self-recrimination. *I knew he was sick. I failed him. If I had loved him more, I would have gone home.* My chest tightens. My head feels cloudy. I sense myself starting to float beyond my body, my go-to survival strategy of dissociation waiting to swoop in.

These are the contextual and content elements of trauma that are so difficult to target in trauma reprocessing. The CASE for trauma, the CASE for survival. All those elements are still floating around in my brain, just waiting for their cue.

Naz had picked the perfect play to challenge the efficacy of Event Havening. He had identified, only if accidentally, an opportunity to address fundamental elements tied to the specific traumatic encodings connected to the night John died. But those SISP neural freeways are still bumper to bumper with guilt, responsibility, shame, aloneness, poor health—all the internal heaviness I've carried for a lifetime.

This new technique we are learning is supposed to address these things. But my skepticism, softened by the outlandishly positive outcome from the day before, has returned in full force.

When it's time to go into our breakout groups, Dr. Steve Ruden approaches me. "Would you like to practice this protocol?"

Looking at him with a mix of gratitude for his consideration and disbelief at what has been suggested in their training session, I swallow hard. "Sure . . . ?"

Finding a quiet space for us, he invites me this time to think about the larger meaning of John's death. I can feel my mind warring with the stories I've been cultivating since he died. The fact is that I have fallen in line with the conviction of both families—John's and my own—that it is not appropriate to discuss the cause of his death. In fact, ten years afterward, his niece, who was there the night he died, will inform me that she still has no idea what actually happened. Our silence aligns with John's own deeply internalized shame about struggling with addiction. The shame that shut down my efforts to get him help while he was alive still holds us all in its grip.

Still, the real John was always the biggest proponent of me telling my recovery story and empowering others through the common connection of our human experiences. I know he would want his story to do the same. But at that moment, I internally buckle under the weight of uncertainty and doubt. *Should I share my real feelings? Or do I only talk about the sadness and the loss that is expected of a widow? Who am I allowed to be?*

Steve seems to understand the battle waging in my soul about what is safe to share. His attunement is both comforting and discomforting—I am being seen in a way I haven't since John died. Once again, that reassuring hand is placed over mine.

"Kate, this is your space. When we lose people we love, there are so many complicated emotions. I can be with all of them if you can."

Staring into his gentle, kind eyes, I know what he says is true. There is no judgment here. This indeed is a safe space—a haven. Suddenly, the name of these techniques makes more sense to me.

Steve begins to use the Havening Techniques with me, this time focused on the CASE for trauma my brain has been building for five years about John's death. My emotions boil over, unleashed by the freedom of the Havening Touch and the change in my brain's electrochemical state. Anger and rage, guilt and shame, followed quickly by anger and rage again. Incredible loss, abandonment, the depths of loneliness. It feels like hours have passed, maybe even a week, but a glance at my watch reveals that just twenty to thirty minutes have gone by. The depth and expansion of emotion in such a short period when given the suitable neurobiological landscape is astounding to me. I can feel my scientific mind hovering above us until, eventually, I swat it away like a fly. I need to experience whatever is to happen, not analyze it.

We complete the Transpirational Havening process in what feels like an epic time-transcending journey; to my surprise, we have some time left. Steve inquires if I would be open to trying something called Outcome Havening, which involves using neuroplasticity to create a new lens for my brain through which to view what happened. Who would say no to that?

I tell him the story of how, one week before John's death, John told me he would probably die young, and how we fought about it afterward. This story contains one of my deepest sources of shame: that I created the opportunity for John to die by not insisting he go into treatment immediately. Recall that when I made that mandate, he left. The door slammed, and he gunned his car fast and furiously away from me. When I took off my engagement ring and placed it on the kitchen counter between us, I drove a wedge between his amygdala's core values for family fealty and our love. And it killed him.

Despite having told this story to almost no one (therapists aside), I still revisit it daily. But never before have I seen with such clarity my shame, my survivor guilt, my felt sense of overwhelming responsibility for not keeping him safe. This is the first time I tell the story without being immersed within those emotions. The CASE crafted by my amygdala has been released. My prefrontal cortex is officially available to bring clarity and with it, absolution. I can feel the truth of what so many therapists have told me for years: There was only so much I could have done. His death was not my fault.

Despite all this development, I do not feel the warmth I had the day before. I don't know where to go in my brain with this experience. Perhaps that's the reason I feel compelled to share it with Steve.

I have to give him credit. He doesn't try to dig deeper into the story or the nuances of what I'm thinking or feeling in that moment, nor does he try to fix my emotional state or give me platitudes about how I did the best I could for John. Instead, he invites me to close my eyes and begin the Havening experience again while he holds space.

Outcome Havening proves to be profound. It is as though I'm tapping into the wisdom and assurance that John tried to give me over the ten years of our relationship. The beliefs he held of who I am as a human. His assurance of my capacity. The gifts of who I am at my core that he always knew and tried to share with me. It turns out the CASE for resilience and thriving has been building in my brain for decades; I just hadn't known how to access it.

I feel a lifetime's worth of shame falling away. The Transpirational Havening protocol goes so far beyond just that night of John's death, beyond the years of living with John as he became sicker and his addiction grew, all the way back into my childhood and the depths of the brokenness that I had been taught was my truth. It is as though all my other therapeutic work across the course of my life is finally synched up and linked in. All the sporadic *Ah-ha!* moments that took place within the daily darkness finally come together as the guiding light, creating a new path for my brain to explore. The feeling is surreal. I've never done psychedelics, but this has to be close.

My mind is blown.

I no longer have to live in fear of my own brain's reactions to the world around me.

I am free.

CHAPTER 21

Healing in Your Hands

"Healing is not just a desired outcome of treatment,
it is a potential that is there from the start. We are wired
to heal, to right ourselves, to grow and transform. This is
not just a metaphor. It is what neuroplasticity is about."

—Hilary Jacobs Hendel

For weeks afterward, I repeatedly wonder whether the changes I felt at *Sleep No More* were simply adrenaline, whether the disintegration of shame and fear in that Transpirational Havening practice will last. Is Amy hiding more sleeper cell grenades? Have the Havening Techniques truly flipped the switch on my past five years of suffering? Am I really free?

The answer is yes. I *am* different. My amygdala is different. Everything is different.

***

On a Tuesday evening, I pack my dogs into my car and set off to visit Naz at his Pasadena home, planning to surprise him with dinner. I pull into the driveway and open the garage door, only to find his car already parked there. *Darn it! Why is he already home?*

I open the door and let the dogs into the house, returning to the car to get my bags. He's not coming to greet me—a conspicuous absence. Naz always greets me at the door, especially when we've been apart for any length of time. Amy starts to go into alert mode.

Returning to the house, I shout out, "Hey Babe?! You home?"

I'm met with silence.

Had this scenario occurred prior to October 25, 2014, a familiar pattern would have hijacked me. I'd have spiraled into a panic and bolted for the stairs and the master bedroom, Amy screaming at me, *He's dead?! Hurry, find him! Maybe you won't be too late this time!*

But here's what happened instead.

Upon being met with silence, Amy's emergency response is shockingly sluggish. Her rapid-fire urgency sounds more like someone mumbling in her sleep. *Quiet. Dead?! Move, lady!* I only get halfway through the first step of my frenzied, PTSD-driven race to the bedroom before the entire pattern collapses. I feel a fizzle in my brain, as though I'm literally sensing the synapses failing to sync into their familiar pattern. Then I burst out laughing as my brain clicks back online: *Oh, yeah, he's at the homeowners' association meeting.* Quick glance at the clock. *He should be home in an hour. Poor guy, he's probably being tortured by that one really controlling neighbor. I should pour him a glass of bourbon for when he gets home.* And then, excitedly, *I can still surprise him with dinner!*

A moment later, it hits me what has just occurred. For years, I've been plagued by the irrational certainty (and the awareness of how irrational it is) that when I don't hear from people, it means they are dead and it is somehow my fault. But this time, there was no irrational trauma spiral, just factual data. Sometimes healing from trauma is just as much about what no longer happens rather than what does.

Dazed, I sink into one of the kitchen chairs, overwhelmed by the enormity of what my brain has just done. What it *hasn't* done. Tinkerbell jumps into my lap and attempts to lick my face while Roscoe burrows his head into my side. It's amazing how animals can sense monumental moments.

The Value of Optimism

That moment of meeting Bill Solz in Jacksonville, Florida, laid the groundwork for my new life, a life free from the painful impacts of trauma that had held me paralyzed for five years, a life with the capacity to start building the treatment team and space that John and I dreamed up together. Newly unencumbered, I begin building a new community in my personal and professional life. But I'm not starting from scratch. Despite the pain rampant in my past, there were also brilliant moments of opportunity and acquired wisdom.

I was nine years old when my grandfather suddenly and unexpectedly died. I had always been so close to Boppie, had always felt deeply loved and accepted by him, a feeling that was rare for me at that point in my life. He listened to me and talked with me. As a little girl, if I spilled orange juice and started to cry, he would spill his too, just to make me feel better. For several years in a row, I spent spring break down in Florida with my Boppie and Nana— the Nana Kay from chapter 2, our fearless Truitt matriarch. The spring before he died, however, I didn't go to Florida as usual, due to a horse show or some other such nonsense. Boppie died that year; I never got to spend more time with him. I was heartbroken. I felt so guilty. Nevertheless, I didn't cry at the funeral. My tender nine-year-old self had already learned tears are weakness and create ample opportunities for bullying.

Father Thom Savage, a dear family friend who led my Boppie's service, asked us grandchildren to write letters about our Boppie. Mine was read in the ceremony; I wrote about how Boppie always gave me riddles. The last one he gave me was, "Is the glass half full or half empty?" An infuriating riddle for a nine-year-old who wanted nothing more than certainty. I pondered the question for a long time and decided that the answer boiled down to circumstance. Even at that tender age, I felt my glass was half empty. Boppie's, I knew, was half full. Based off my letter, Father Thom talked about how Boppie always showed us how to live life by being half full.

I often think back to Boppie and his glass-half-full approach to life. His realistic optimism was not naivete, not forgetting the past like it never happened. Rather, it was a choice to build his life around a core of hope and trust.

Having a sense of realistic optimism is an important part of developing an empowered CASE for thriving. This involves believing that there is possibility and opportunity in every difficult moment while concurrently knowing that the wisdom of each hard moment will be revealed in time. This belief isn't something we must be born with; it's a skill we have to practice. Resilience and agency offer a framework for training our brains to see the world with a half-full glass.

Moving Forward With Resilience

Newly freed from the fear of being activated into a trauma vortex, thanks to my transformative experience in New York, I joyfully return to clinical practice. One day glows in my memory with special clarity, a day when the seeds for a personally empowered, neuroplasticity-based resilient brain care program that had been growing in my mind burst into life. It was the day I began work with a new patient—a fellow psychotherapist, in fact. I only saw her for two sessions. The first was spent depotentiating an acutely traumatic experience: she had been assaulted leaving work one day, resulting in a week-long hospitalization. The perpetrator was never apprehended, which left her terrified to leave her home. By three months after the assault, this very understandable fear had morphed into severe agoraphobia. Just thinking about leaving her home sent her into panic attacks, sometimes four or five a day.

I open my office door to greet the patient and find her huddled in a chair at the far end of the reception area. I note that she has moved the chair into a corner from which she can vigilantly track all coming and going through the office doors.

At the time, my offices were in a historic building in the heart of Old Town Pasadena—great location, gorgeous architecture, but the soundproofing from the street to our second-story reception area definitely left something to be desired. We compensated for the ambient street sounds with white noise machines and soothing meditation music. But before I can even welcome the new patient, a cacophony rises from the street below—loud masculine yells followed by an even louder crash.

As the sound explodes into the room, I witness the patient's amygdala's CASE for trauma in action. Her entire body jerks inward, pulling her into a small ball in the chair. Her eyes meet mine for a fleeting moment, filled with fear, before they slam shut and her forehead drops to her knees. Her fists ball up and a guttural groan of psychic pain crosses the threshold between us.

My brain flashes back to my own devastating experience with Therapist X; in response, I'm filled with an almost maternal sense of protection and determination. So clear are the words in my mind that I almost worry I've spoken them out loud: *No way. Not on my watch, Amy.*

The sound is over as abruptly as it began; in odd contrast, there now seems to be laughter wafting up from the street. I take a few careful steps into the room.

"Hey . . . may I get you some water or tea?"

At my gentle inquiry, her head lifts and her cheeks flush red—Amy's tide of shame and embarrassment arriving right on schedule. Remembering that the patient shared in her consult that she was a huge Star Wars fan, I offer a humorous redirect: "The force is clearly strong with your amygdala."

Her face registers surprise and lights up with a small smile of relief. She expels the breath she had been holding and slowly makes her way to her feet. "I'm sorry, Dr. Kate, I don't know what's wrong with me. I'm losing my mind."

"Please don't apologize," I say as I motion her toward my office. "Your brain is working hard to keep you safe. Sometimes our brains just do really weird things. Come on in. Water or tea?"

She smiles gratefully and motions to a water bottle sticking out of her bag. "I brought my own." Entering my office, she glances over her shoulder at me. "Now tell me about how *that* reaction is my brain trying to keep me safe. I don't buy it."

I grin, we get settled, and I start the session by sharing a summary of what is happening in her brain (introducing her to Amy the amygdala) and explain a bit about EMLIs. I then introduce her to the Havening Touch and prepare her to begin the Havening trauma reprocessing protocols. As we begin the work, I invite her to briefly focus on the experience of the assault, an exposure designed to shift the amygdala into a state of activation. Calling the experience to mind instantly returns her to the pale, tense, and trembling state I originally saw in my waiting room. Gently, I invite her to assess her activation using the 0-to-10-point SUD scale.* After a moment of trembling in my chair, she meekly reports, "I'm at 100."

Knowing all too well what that means, my heart aches even more intensely for the pain she is living within. I immediately guide her through the same Event Havening protocol that gave me my own brain back just six months prior and am delighted to observe her nervous system growing relaxed and calm within a matter of minutes. Twenty-five minutes later, when she goes to check in on the memory of the assault, it has lost its charge. She even locates herself on the SUD scale as 0. The memory is still there, but the terror is gone. The change, and her relief, are palpable. The vise grip of tension that held her captive is gone. Her breath, once shallow, now flows freely and easily.

At the close of the session, she asks me, "How are you bringing this to the world?"

"I'm doing everything I can," I reply with conviction. I share how I am bringing this work into almost every session with the forty patients I see each week, how I am beginning to work alongside the creators of the Havening Techniques, how I am continuing to deepen and refine my NeuroTriad approach to treatment.

She looks me square in the eye. "You have to do more," she says. "If I hadn't found you, I would have killed myself."

Her words strike a deep chord within me, resurfacing memories of my own struggles. I know what it's like to lose oneself to trauma, darkness, and pain. I know how easily they can steal life away. I breathe; then, with a gentle nod, I reassure her, "I will."

---

* The Subjective Units of Distress Scale (SUDS) is the measure of the felt level of a person's distress from 0 to 10, with 0 being totally calm and 10 being out of control—the most stress and anxiety the person has ever experienced.

Her words stay with me after she leaves. *Do more.* Leaning back in my office chair, I stare thoughtfully at my bookcase. What had I most needed in those darkest moments when my amygdala overwhelmed me with trauma or panic? Or worse, plagued me with suicidal thoughts? Even back then, I had so much knowledge, years of specialized training—what could have helped me access it?

My eyes fall on the tattered spine of my decades-old copy of *Man's Search for Meaning.* A quote that has often been attributed to the book's author, the late Austrian neurologist, psychiatrist, and philosopher Viktor Frankl, springs to mind: "Between stimulus and response, there is a space. In that space is our power to choose our response. In our response lies our growth and our freedom."

In my darkest moments, I needed space from the pain. A space to breathe, even just for a moment. My brain needed the room to believe that something else could be possible, something worth the struggle to keep breathing. *What if Havening is the key to creating this neurobiological space?*

***

The patient's second session was a follow-up visit. This was unique, as patients who have a single incident event like hers often cancel their follow-up after a Havening reprocessing session because they simply don't need it. Upon her arrival, we checked in about how she was feeling and what her symptoms were. She said everything was better. Her panic attacks were gone. She had withdrawn her disability application, and she was back at work. She told me she had even been out to a comedy club and felt completely fine—in fact, she had fun!

But then, her tone turning somber, she told me the reason for her follow-up visit.

"I want to better understand my brain. The assault was awful, but what happened next—my own brain trying to destroy me—that was terrifying."

I felt tears come to my eyes and I'm sure my hand fluttered to my chest, covering my heart. I knew how she felt.

She continued, "Help me understand how this happened to me, and how I can make sure it never happens again. I might get assaulted again—it could happen—and I refuse to not live my life."

Out of the corner of my eye, I still see Viktor Frankl's book on my shelf. My brain flashes back to when I first saw it—maybe twelve or thirteen years old, wandering through one of my favorite hideouts, a local antique store in Kansas. I was immediately drawn to the title. I had a deep desire to understand why I was in so much pain, why I struggled with such dark thoughts. I was searching for meaning and the book's title called out to me with the promise of an answer or, at least, a reassurance that I was not alone.

The mantra that haunted me since John's death once again comes to mind: *There has to be meaning in this.* Until now, I hadn't realized how long those words had been a guiding force in my life. Perhaps this is why my story has unfolded in its particular way. Perhaps my brain can serve as an educational opportunity for others. Perhaps this is the "more" that I can do.

We talk through her specific areas of vulnerability based on her brain's developmental story, exploring how she can build mental resilience while making sure her landscape isn't permissive toward carrying and encoding trauma. She is eager to do whatever it might take to solidify and strengthen the powerful impact of our previous session. Together, we come up with a tailor-made brain health program, starting with a "Distraction Inventory" (as we call it) of safe brain games that she can use while applying the Self-Havening

Touch to proactively calm and regulate her nervous system. Armed with tools she can use on her own, anytime and anywhere, she can be confident that her brain won't encode and carry negative experiences forward.

This session reignites an important drive that has inspired my work almost since it began: to help people separate their brain from their mind and Self. Our chaotic, painful, messy human moments are not who we are; rather, they are a part of how our brains have learned to help us keep breathing. The session also highlights the necessity of expanding this information beyond my individual clinical care. I start to imagine a world where we empower people to heal themselves, continually decrease stress and anxiety, manage their moods, and increase their resilience. Taking it a step further, I imagine training others—my colleagues, community leaders, teachers, parents, and more—in these self-healing abilities. Thanks to that client's inspiration, my Resilient Brain Model begins to take on a new expansiveness. Today, we call these self-healing and empowerment programs *Healing in Your Hands*.

Beyond Survival

My favorite definition of resilience comes from Rick Hanson (2018), one of the greatest minds in neuroplasticity and brain resilience: "Resilience is the capacity to recover from adversity and pursue our goals despite challenges."

It's simple, but easier said than done. Resilience requires intentionally leaning back into your life after a challenge to keep moving forward and pursue your goals. Intention is key. Whether we already have a sense of purpose or we create one by continually choosing to draw our next breath, purpose is key to resilience. If we have purpose, we can overcome.

There is a second part to Hanson's (2018) definition of resilience, and it explains what resilience does: "It helps us survive the worst day of our life and thrive every day of our life." Survive and thrive—important distinctions. I survived my trauma, and I want people to know how I was able to do that. But a good life is about much more than surviving, and thriving can only happen inside a resilient brain. Resilience is a proactive participation in how the brain is functioning. To participate effectively, you first have to understand what is happening within that three-pound ball of goo sitting in our heads. As Sir Francis Bacon (and later Schoolhouse Rock) reminds us, "Knowledge is power."

Today, we have that knowledge. We can empower people with tools to manage their emotions and create new neural pathways for personal empowerment. We truly carry the power of healing in our hands because of the brain's ability to change through neuroplasticity. The brain continually changes itself over time, and we can help it along in the directions we want it to go by repeatedly stimulating specific pathways, such as *calm, content, motivated.* We now have and can teach the tools for creating a resilient brain and address anxiety, enhance learning capacity, and even heal through the difficulties of daily life. All of it is in our hands.

CHAPTER 22

Coming Home to Self

"The human psyche, like human bones,
is strongly inclined towards self-healing."

—Sir John Bowlby

t's a bright and sunny California morning. I'm on my way to my offices in Pasadena, California. I'm looking forward to another full day of spending time with my team and a long list of scheduled meetings with colleagues and thought leaders who are also endeavoring to put the power of healing into our own hands. I'm on the phone with Dr. Ronald Ruden, debriefing about the exciting week we just shared in New York City, where I was invited to present at the United Nation's Commission on the Status of Women. To say my life has expanded and transformed in incredible ways is an understatement. The me that arrived at Naz's house to make him dinner in November of 2014 would never have been able to imagine what I have become, but she certainly would have hoped, and I know she would be so proud of each step taken, each challenge met.

Rebuilding Your World

In 2014, my amygdala began its journey of healing. The ten years since then have brought incredible joy, exciting discoveries, deeply satisfying successes. They've also brought challenges, failures, and even new griefs. Even as I savor the daily delight of my marriage and watch my clinical practice expand in ways I never expected, I still deal with the lingering impact of encephalitis and navigate thorny relationships with family and loved ones.

There's no magic wand that can be waved to "fix" everything that trauma has taken from us. Change takes time and effort. However, when we stop fighting against the amygdala and instead partner with it, the effort is much less and the rewards are much greater. As you learned back in chapter 13, the brain is designed to build your world through each experience that links into your core survival values as well as the meaning you've made of those experiences. Making meaning around fear, scarcity, and bare survival is only natural—it's a primal instinct developed over thousands of years of humans running for their lives. But you can change the pattern of how your brain makes meaning by moving into an intentional relationship with your neurobiology and the experiences that have shaped it. As I tell my patients, we turn to the past to learn, not return.

Many things in life will happen whether you want them to or not. What you control is how you show up for yourself within the experiences and, often more importantly, in the aftermath. Don't ignore your past or try to forget or deny it. Lean into self-compassion for what happened to you then because it's what got you here. As the philosopher Søren Kierkegaard (1843) wrote, "Life can only be understood backwards; but it must be lived forwards."

As the phoenix story shows, there's no single moment of rising from the ashes to a new life of triumph over trauma. Like any relationship, this intentional partnership with your brain is a lifelong process, one that develops with every new (or old) challenge you encounter. However, it takes just one small, simple act to begin this relationship. It happens when you stop running from the threats your brain is trained to perceive and allow yourself to feel proud of the fact that *you have survived.* It takes grit, perseverance, and drive to keep breathing, especially when you have endured deeply painful experiences. If you're still here, you have what it takes to heal.

Knowing this opens the door to something even more healing: the discovery of your purpose. For trauma survivors, the power of purpose is profound. For some, it comes easily, an intrinsic knowledge of what they must do. For others, like me, it comes from profound tragedy chased by an internal awareness that there is meaning to it all.

The truth is that my ability to rise from the ashes began long before this five-year journey through traumatic grief. While I didn't know it at the time, I was growing my phoenix wings throughout my life, each experience of pain and loneliness and self-worth increasing my brain's resilience and determination to survive. Recognizing this is, I believe, the secret to conscious recovery and resilience. Sharing this secret is the purpose that anchors me each time I feel the flames approaching. Knowing what my brain is capable of, I have confidence that I will rise again.

Shine On

John helped me lay an original foundation for how to believe in myself. With his death, I was challenged to create a new and truly resilient construct of Self that had the grit, agency, and capacity to build the life I wanted to live.

That doesn't mean that my present moment is not being informed 90 percent by my past. I know that it is because that is the way the brain is designed. But through intentional attention and the opportunity of neuroplasticity, I have been able to transform my CASE for survival into one for thriving. I have a new CASE for Self, one that I am consciously and proactively creating to replace the one created by the pain and traumas of my past. I have been able to help my amygdala heal through the painful experiences from the past and change the freeways and frameworks around those experiences. In my dark moments, I return to the phoenix, the symbol of resilience and internal resource that arose from the ashes of my devastating experiences. Now I choose to fly into the flames, knowing I'm able to focus that attentional spotlight in my brain to find the wisdom within them.

You may not feel it yet, but you have the same power within yourself. Your brain, your body, your heart, your own hands—they hold everything you need to remake the meaning of your story. I hope that if you've learned one thing from my journey, it's that the deepest tragedies create space for the most empowered growth. Never underestimate your ability to experience the darkness and still shine on.

References

American Psychiatric Association. (2013). *Diagnostic and statistical manual of mental disorders* (5th ed.). https://doi.org/10.1176/appi.books.9780890425596

Ansell, E. B., Rando, K., Tuit, K., Guarnaccia, J., & Sinha, R. (2012). Cumulative adversity and smaller gray matter volume in medial prefrontal, anterior cingulate, and insula regions. *Biological Psychiatry, 72*(1), 57–64. https://doi.org/10.1016/j.biopsych.2011.11.022

Arain, M., Haque, M., Johal, L., Mathur, P., Nel, W., Rais, A., Sandhu, R., & Sharma, S. (2013). Maturation of the adolescent brain. *Neuropsychiatric Disease and Treatment, 9,* 449–461. https://doi.org/10.2147/NDT.S39776

Ballard, E. D., Gilbert, J. R., Fields, J. S., Nugent, A. C., & Zarate, C. A., Jr. (2020). Network changes in insula and amygdala connectivity accompany implicit suicidal associations. *Frontiers in Psychiatry, 11*(577628). https://doi.org/10.3389/fpsyt.2020.577628

Baratta, M. V., Christianson, J. P., Gómez, D. M., Zarza, C. M., Amat, J., Masini, C. V., Watkins, L. R., & Maier, S. F. (2007). Controllable versus uncontrollable stressors bi-directionally modulate conditioned but not innate fear. *Neuroscience, 146*(4), 1495–1503. https://doi.org/10.1016/j.neuroscience.2007.03.042

Bartels, A., & Zeki, S. (2004). The neural correlates of maternal and romantic love. *NeuroImage, 21*(3), 1155–1166. https://doi.org/10.1016/j.neuroimage.2003.11.003

Brandão, M. L., & Lovick, T. A. (2019). Role of the dorsal periaqueductal gray in posttraumatic stress disorder: Mediation by dopamine and neurokinin. *Translational Psychiatry, 9*(1), 232. https://doi.org/10.1038/s41398-019-0565-8

Breslau, N. (2001). The epidemiology of posttraumatic stress disorder: What is the extent of the problem? *Journal of Clinical Psychiatry, 62*(Suppl. 17), 16–22.

Brewin, C. R., Andrews, B., & Valentine, J. D. (2000). Meta-analysis of risk factors for posttraumatic stress disorder in trauma-exposed adults. *Journal of Consulting and Clinical Psychology, 68*(5), 748–766. https://doi.org/10.1037//0022-006x.68.5.748

Brooks, A. W. (2014). Get excited: Reappraising pre-performance anxiety as excitement. *Journal of Experimental Psychology: General, 143*(3), 1144–1158. https://doi.org/10.1037/a0035325

Brown, B. (2007). *I thought it was just me (but it isn't): Making the journey from "What will people think?" to "I am enough."* Avery.

Brown, B. (2010). *The gifts of imperfection.* Hazelden Publishing.

Brown, B. (2012). *Daring greatly: How the courage to be vulnerable transforms the way we live, love, parent, and lead.* Gotham Books.

Brown, B. (2013). *Shame vs. guilt.* https://brenebrown.com/articles/2013/01/15/shame-v-guilt/

Burke Harris, N. (2014). *How childhood trauma affects health across a lifetime* [Video]. TED Conferences. https://www.ted.com/talks/nadine_burke_harris_how_childhood_trauma_affects_health_across_a_lifetime

Centers for Disease Control and Prevention. (2019, November). Adverse childhood experiences (ACEs): Preventing early trauma to improve health. *CDC VitalSigns.* https://www.cdc.gov/vitalsigns/aces/pdf/vs-1105-aces-H.pdf

Chaves, J. F., & Brown, J. M. (1987). Spontaneous cognitive strategies for the control of clinical pain and stress. *Journal of Behavioral Medicine, 10*(3), 263–276. https://doi.org/10.1007/BF00846540

Choi, C. (2007, March 15). Fact or fiction?: A cockroach can live without its head. *Scientific American.* https://www.scientificamerican.com/article/fact-or-fiction-cockroach-can-live-without-head/

Corchs, F., & Schiller, D. (2019). Threat-related disorders as persistent motivational states of defense. *Current Opinion in Behavioral Sciences, 26*, 62–68. https://doi.org/10.1016/j.cobeha.2018.10.007

Cozolino, L. J. (2016). *Why therapy works: using our minds to change our brains* (1st ed.). W. W. Norton & Company.

Cunningham, W. A., & Brosch, T. (2012). Motivational salience: Amygdala tuning from traits, needs, values, and goals. *Current Directions in Psychological Science, 21*(1), 54–59. https://doi.org/10.1177/0963721411430832

Cunningham, W. A., & Kirkland, T. (2013). The joyful, yet balanced, amygdala: Moderated responses to positive but not negative stimuli in trait happiness. *Social Cognitive and Affective Neuroscience, 9*(6), 760–766. https://doi.org/10.1093/scan/nst045

Dalgleish, T., & Power, M. J. (2004). The I of the storm—Relations between self and conscious emotion experience: Comment on Lambie and Marcel (2002). *Psychological Review, 111*(3), 812–818. https://doi.org/10.1037/0033-295X.111.3.812

Easton, A. (2022). Death from encephalitis (acute stage). *The Encephalitis Society.* https://www.encephalitis.info/Handlers/Download.ashx?IDMF=8eedc173-6ae1-4fd6-8f7e-7616dee7ee03

Ehlers, A., & Clark, D. M. (2000). A cognitive model of posttraumatic stress disorder. *Behaviour Research and Therapy, 38*(4), 319–345. https://doi.org/10.1016/s0005-7967(99)00123-0

Emerson, R. W. (2003). Self reliance. In N. Baym (Ed.), *The Norton anthology of American literature* (6th ed., pp. 1160–1176). W. W. Norton & Company.

Evans, A. R., Daly, E. S., Catlett, K. K., Paul, K. S., King, S. J., Skinner, M. M., Neese, H. P., Hublin, J. J., Townsend, G. C., Schwartz, G. T., & Jernvall, J. (2016). A simple rule governs the evolution and development of hominin tooth size. *Nature 530,* 477–480. https://doi.org/10.1038/nature16972

Felliti, V. J., Anda, R. F., Nordenberg, D., Williamson, D. F., Spitz, A. M., Edwards, V., Koss, M. P., & Marks, J. S. (1998). Relationship of childhood abuse and household dysfunction to many of the leading causes of death in adults. The Adverse Childhood Experiences (ACE) Study. *American Journal of Preventative Medicine, 14,* 245–258. http://doi.org/10.1016/s0749-3797(98)00017-8

Felmingham, K. L., Bryant, R. A., & Evian, G. (2003). Processing angry and neutral faces in post-traumatic stress disorder: An event-related potentials study. *NeuroReport, 14*(5), 777–780. https://doi.org/10.1097/00001756-200304150-00024

Fernando, A. B. P., Murray, J. E., & Milton, A. L. (2013). The amygdala: Securing pleasure and avoiding pain. *Frontiers in Behavioral Neuroscience, 7,* 190. https://doi.org/10.3389/fnbeh.2013.00190

Foa, E. B., & Kozak M. J. (1986). Emotional processing of fear: Exposure to corrective information. *Psychological Bulletin, 99*, 20–35. https://pubmed.ncbi.nlm.nih.gov/2871574/

Fox, V., Dalman, C., Dal, H., Hollander, A. C., Kirkbride, J. B., & Pitman, A. (2021). Suicide risk in people with post-traumatic stress disorder: A cohort study of 3.1 million people in Sweden. *Journal of Affective Disorders, 279*, 609–616. https://doi.org/10.1016/j.jad.2020.10.009

Frick, A., Björkstrand, J., Lubberink, M., Eriksson, A., Fredrikson, M., & Åhs, F. (2022). Dopamine and fear memory formation in the human amygdala. *Molecular Psychiatry, 27*(3), 1704–1711. https://doi.org/10.1038/s41380-021-01400-x

George, D., & Blieck, A. (2011). Rise of the earliest tetrapods: An early Devonian origin from marine environment. *PloS One, 6*(7), e22136. https://doi.org/10.1371/journal.pone.0022136

Gibson, E. J., & Walk, R. D. (1960). The "visual cliff." *Scientific American, 202*, 64–71. https://doi.org/10.1038/scientificamerican0460-64

Giedd, J. N., Blumenthal, J., Jeffries, N. O., Castellanos, F. X., Liu, H., Zijdenbos, A., Paus, T., Evans, A. C., & Rapoport, J. L. (1999). Brain development during childhood and adolescence: A longitudinal MRI study. *Nature Neuroscience, 2*(10), 861–863. https://doi.org/10.1038/13158

Gieler, U., & Gieler, T. (2020). Suicidal risk with isotretinoin treatment – A never-ending story. *Journal of the European Academy of Dermatology and Venereology, 34*(6), 1131–1133. https://doi.org/10.1111/jdv.16489

Goldstein, R. B., Smith, S. M., Chou, S. P., Saha, T. D., Jung, J., Zhang, H., Pickering, R. P., Ruan, W. J., Huang, B., & Grant, B. F. (2016). The epidemiology of DSM-5 posttraumatic stress disorder in the United States: Results from the National Epidemiologic Survey on Alcohol and Related Conditions-III. *Social Psychiatry and Psychiatric Epidemiology, 51*(8), 1137–1148. https://doi.org/10.1007/s00127-016-1208-5

Grupe, D. W., & Nitschke, J. B. (2013). Uncertainty and anticipation in anxiety: an integrated neurobiological and psychological perspective. Nature reviews. *Neuroscience, 14*(7), 488–501. https://doi.org/10.1038/nrn3524

Guex, R., Méndez-Bértolo, C., Moratti, S., Strange, B. A., Spinelli, L., Murray, R. J., Sander, D., Seeck, M., Vuilleumier, P., & Domínguez-Borràs, J. (2020). Temporal dynamics of amygdala response to emotion- and action-relevance. *Scientific Reports, 10*(11138). https://doi.org/10.1038/s41598-020-67862-1

Hamann, S., Ely, T. D., Grafton, S. T., & Kilts, C. D. (1999). Amygdala activity related to enhanced memory for pleasant and aversive stimuli. *Nature Neuroscience, 2*, 289–293. https://doi.org/10.1038/6404

Hanson, R. (2018, April 21). *Walking evenly over uneven ground: Using positive neuroplasticity to cultivate resilient well-being.* [Slides]. https://s3.us-west-1.amazonaws.com/media.rickhanson.net/slides/TrueNorthInsight04.21.18.pdf

Harari, Y. N. (2015). *Sapiens: A brief history of humankind.* Harper.

Harricharan, S., Rabellino, D., Frewen, P. A., Densmore, M., Théberge, J., McKinnon, M. C., Schore, A. N., & Lanius, R. A. (2016). fMRI functional connectivity of the periaqueductal gray in PTSD and its dissociative subtype. *Brain and Behavior, 6*(12), e00579. https://doi.org/10.1002/brb3.579

Herculano-Houzel, S. (2012). The remarkable, yet not extraordinary, human brain as a scaled-up primate brain and its associated cost. *Proceedings of the National Academy of Sciences, 109*(Suppl. 1), 10661–10668. https://doi.org/10.1073/pnas.1201895109

Horowitz, M. J. (2011). *Stress response syndromes: PTSD, grief, adjustment, and dissociative disorders* (5th ed.). Jason Aronson.

Hughes, K., Bellis, M. A., Hardcastle, K. A., Sethi, D., Butchart, A., Mikton, C., Jones, L., & Dunne, M. P. (2017). The effect of multiple adverse childhood experiences on health: A systematic review and meta-analysis. *The Lancet Public Health, 2*(8), e356–e366. https://doi.org/10.1016/S2468-2667(17)30118-4

Hur, J., Smith, J. F., DeYoung, K. A., Anderson, A. S., Kuang, J., Kim, H. C., Tillman, R. M., Kuhn, M., Fox, A. S., & Shackman, A. J. (2020). Anxiety and the neurobiology of temporally uncertain threat anticipation. *The Journal of Neuroscience, 40*(41), 7949–7964. https://doi.org/10.1523/JNEUROSCI.0704-20.2020

Jamieson, J. P., Nock, M. K., & Mendes, W. B. (2012). Mind over matter: Reappraising arousal improves cardiovascular and cognitive responses to stress. *Journal of Experimental Psychology: General, 141*(3), 417–422. https://doi.org/10.1037/a0025719

Janak, P. H., & Tye, K. M. (2015). From circuits to behaviour in the amygdala. *Nature, 517*(7534), 284–292. https://doi.org/10.1038/nature14188

Junger, S. (2016). *Tribe: On homecoming and belonging.* Twelve.

Junger, S. (2018, April 2). The anthropology of manhood. *National Review.* https://www.nationalreview.com/magazine/2018/03/15/why-are-men-violent-science-society/

Kessler, R. C., Sonnega, A., Bromet, E., Hughes, M., & Nelson, C. B. (1995). Posttraumatic stress disorder in the National Comorbidity Survey. *Archives of General Psychiatry, 52*(12), 1048–1060. https://www.doi.org/10.1001/archpsyc.1995.03950240066012

Kierkegaard, S. (1843). Søren Kierkegaards Skrifter, Journalen JJ:167, *Søren Kierkegaard Research Center, 18*, 306.

Kikuchi, Y., Matsutani, Y., Mori, K., Hanada, K., Shirakawa, Y., Shirato, M., & Noriuchi, M. (2018). Brainstem activity predicts attachment-related anxiety. *Neuropsychiatry, 8*(1), 324–334. https://www.jneuropsychiatry.org/peer-review/brainstem-activity-predicts-attachmentrelated-anxiety-12375.html

Kochanek, K. D., Xu, J., Murphy, S. L., Miniño, A. M., Kung H. C. (2011). Deaths: Preliminary data for 2009, *National Vital Statistics Reports, 59*(4), 1–51. https://pubmed.ncbi.nlm.nih.gov/25073815/

Krause-Utz, A., Frost, R., Winter, D., & Elzinga, B. M. (2017). Dissociation and alterations in brain function and structure: Implications for borderline personality disorder. *Current Psychiatry Reports, 19*(6). https://doi.org/10.1007/s11920-017-0757-y

Lancel, M., van Marle, H. J. F., Van Veen, M. M., & van Schagen, A. M. (2021). Disturbed sleep in PTSD: Thinking beyond nightmares. *Frontiers in Psychiatry, 12*(767760). https://doi.org/10.3389/fpsyt.2021.767760

Lanius, R. A., Vermetten, E., Loewenstein, R. J., Brand, B., Schmahl, C., Bremner, J. D., & Spiegel, D. (2010). Emotion modulation in PTSD: Clinical and neurobiological evidence for a dissociative subtype. *The*

American Journal of Psychiatry, 167(6), 640–647. https://doi.org/10
.1176/appi.ajp.2009.09081168

LeDoux, J. E. (2012). Evolution of human emotion: A view through fear.
Progress in Brain Research, 195, 431–442. https://doi.org/10.1016
/B978-0-444-53860-4.00021-0

Leite, L., Esper, N. B., Junior, J. R. M. L., Lara, D. R., & Buchweitz, A.
(2022). An exploratory study of resting-state functional connectivity of
amygdala subregions in posttraumatic stress disorder following trauma
in adulthood. *Scientific Reports, 12*(1), 9558. https://doi.org/10.1038
/s41598-022-13395-8

Lethem, J., Slade, P.D., Troup, J. D. G., & Bentley, G. (1983). Outline
of fear-avoidance model of exaggerated pain perceptions. *Behaviour
Research and Therapy, 21*(4), 401–408. https://doi.org/10.1016/0005
-7967(83)90009-8

Lissek, S., Powers, A. S., McClure, E. B., Phelps, E. A., Woldehawariat,
G., Grillon, C., & Pine, D. S. (2005, November). Classical fear
conditioning in the anxiety disorders: a meta-analysis. *Behaviour
Research and Therapy, 43*(11), 1391–1424. https://doi.org/10.1016/j
.brat.2004.10.007

Mateos-Aparicio, P., & Rodríguez-Moreno, A. (2019). The impact of
studying brain plasticity. *Frontiers in Cellular Neuroscience, 13(66).*
https://doi.org/10.3389/fncel.2019.00066

McEwen, B. S. (2019). What is the confusion with cortisol? *Chronic Stress, 3.*
https://doi.org/10.1177/2470547019833647

McEwen, B. S., & Akil, H. (2020). Revisiting the stress concept:
Implications for affective disorders. *Journal of Neuroscience, 40*(1),
12–21. https://doi.org/10.1523/JNEUROSCI.0733-19.2019

McLaughlin, K. A., Koenen, K. C., Hill, E. D., Petukhova, M., Sampson,
N. A., Zaslavsky, A. M., & Kessler, R. C. (2013). Trauma exposure and
posttraumatic stress disorder in a national sample of adolescents. *Journal
of the American Academy of Child and Adolescent Psychiatry, 52*(8), 815–
830.e14. https://doi.org/10.1016/j.jaac.2013.05.011

Méndez-Bértolo, C., Moratti, S., Toledano, R., Lopez-Sosa, F., Martínez-
Alvarez, R., Mah, Y. H., Vuilleumier, P., Gil-Nagel, A., & Strange, B. A.
(2016). A fast pathway for fear in human amygdala. *Nature Neuroscience,
19*(8), 1041–1049. https://doi.org/10.1038/nn.4324

Merrick, M. T., Ford, D. C., Ports, K. A., Guinn, A. S., Chen, J., Klevens, J., Metzler, M., Jones, C. M., Simon, T. R., Daniel, V. M., Ottley, P., & Mercy, J. A. (2019). Vital signs: Estimated proportion of adult health problems attributable to adverse childhood experiences and implications for prevention – 25 states, 2015–2017. *Morbidity and Mortality Weekly Report, 68*(44), 999–1005. https://doi.org/10.15585/mmwr.mm6844e1

Mokhtar, M., & Singh, P. (2022). "Neuroanatomy, periaqueductal gray." In *StatPearls*. StatPearls Publishing. https://www.ncbi.nlm.nih.gov /books/NBK554391/

Moriarty, O., McGuire, B. E., & Finn, D. P. (2011). The effect of pain on cognitive function: A review of clinical and preclinical research. *Progress in Neurobiology, 93*(3), 385–404. https://doi.org/10.1016/j.pneurobio .2011.01.002

Mueller-Pfeiffer, C., Schick, M., Schulte-Vels, T., O'Gorman, R., Michels, L., Martin-Soelch, C., Blair, J. R., Rufer, M., Schnyder, U., Zeffiro, T., & Hasler, G. (2013). Atypical visual processing in posttraumatic stress disorder. *NeuroImage: Clinical, 3*, 531–538. https://doi.org/10.1016/j .nicl.2013.08.009

Nelson, C. A., Bhutta, Z. A., Harris, N. B., Danese, A., & Samara, M. (2020). Adversity in childhood is linked to mental and physical health throughout life. *BMJ, 371*, m3048. https://doi.org/10.1136/bmj.m3048

O'Connor, M. (2022). *The grieving brain: The surprising science of how we learn from love and loss.* Harper One.

O'Keefe, J. (1976). Place units in the hippocampus of the freely moving rat. *Experimental Neurology, 51*(1), 78–109. https://doi.org/10.1016/0014 -4886(76)90055-8

O'Keefe, J. (2014, December 7). Nobel lecture: Spatial cells in the hippocampal formation. *The Nobel Foundation.* https://www.nobelprize .org/uploads/2018/06/okeefe-lecture.pdf

Oya, H., Kawasaki, H., Howard, M. A. III, & Adolphs, R. (2002). Electrophysiological responses in the human amygdala discriminate emotion categories of complex visual stimuli. *Journal of Neuroscience, 22*(21), 9502–9512. https://doi.org/10.1523/JNEUROSCI.22-21 -09502.2002

Ozer, E. J., Best, S. R., Lipsey, T. L., & Weiss, D. S. (2003). Predictors of posttraumatic stress disorder and symptoms in adults: A meta-analysis.

Psychological Bulletin, 129(1), 52–73. https://doi.org/10.1037/0033
-2909.129.1.52

Payne, W. N., De Jesus, O., & Payne, A. N. (2023). Contrecoup brain
injury. In *StatPearls*. StatPearls Publishing. https://www.ncbi.nlm.nih
.gov/books/NBK536965/

Petrini, L., & Arendt-Nielsen, L. (2020). Understanding pain
catastrophizing: Putting pieces together. *Frontiers in Psychology,
11*(603420). https://doi.org/10.3389/fpsyg.2020.603420

Phelps, E. A., Lempert, K. M., & Sokol-Hessner, P. (2014). Emotion and
decision making: Multiple modulatory neural circuits. *Annual Review of
Neuroscience, 37*, 263–287. https://doi.org/10.1146/annurev-neuro
-071013-014119

Pietrzak, R. H., Goldstein, R. B., Southwick, S. M., & Grant, B. F. (2011).
Prevalence and Axis I comorbidity of full and partial posttraumatic
stress disorder in the United States: results from Wave 2 of the National
Epidemiologic Survey on Alcohol and Related Conditions. *Journal of
Anxiety Disorders, 25*(3), 456–465. https://doi.org/10.1016/j.janxdis
.2010.11.010

Powell, A., Shennan, S., & Thomas, M. G. (2009). Late Pleistocene
demography and the appearance of modern human behavior. *Science,
324*(5932), 1298–1301. https://doi.org/10.1126/science.1170165

Qasim, S. E., Miller, J., Inman, C. S., Gross, R. E., Willie, J. T., Lega, B.,
Lin, J. J., Sharan, A., Wu, C., Sperling, M. R., Sheth, S. A., McKhann,
G. M., Smith, E. H., Schevon, C., Stein, J. M., & Jacobs, J. (2019).
Memory retrieval modulates spatial tuning of single neurons in the
human entorhinal cortex. *Nature Neuroscience, 22*(12), 2078–2086.
https://doi.org/10.1038/s41593-019-0523-z

Quartana, P. J., Campbell, C. M., & Edwards, R. R. (2009). Pain
catastrophizing: A critical review. *Expert Review of Neurotherapeutics,
9*(5), 745–758. https://doi.org/10.1586/ern.09.34

Quinn, K., Boone, L., Scheidell, J. D., Mateu-Gelabert, P., McGorray, S. P.,
Beharie, N., Cottler, L. B., & Khan, M. R. (2016). The relationships of
childhood trauma and adulthood prescription pain reliever misuse and
injection drug use. *Drug and Alcohol Dependence, 169*, 190–198. https://
doi.org/10.1016/j.drugalcdep.2016.09.021

Repovs, G., & Baddeley, A. (2006). The multi-component model of working memory: Explorations in experimental cognitive psychology. *Neuroscience, 139*(1), 5–21. https://doi.org/10.1016/j.neuroscience .2005.12.061

Rozin, P., & Royzman, E. B. (2001). Negativity bias, negativity dominance, and contagion. *Personality and Social Psychology Review, 5*(4), 296–320. https://doi.org/10.1207/S15327957PSPR0504_2

Ruden, R. A. (2011). *When the past is always present: Emotional traumatization, causes, and cures.* Taylor & Francis Group.

Ruden, R. A. (2018). Harnessing electroceuticals to treat disorders arising from traumatic stress: Theoretical considerations using a psychosensory model. *EXPLORE, 15*(3), 222–229. https://doi.org/10.1016/j.explore .2018.05.005

SAMHSA Trauma and Justice Strategic Initiative. (2014, July). *SAMHSA's concept of trauma and guidance for a trauma-informed approach.* [Slides]. U.S. Department of Health and Human Services Substance Abuse and Mental Health Services Administration. https://store.samhsa.gov/sites /default/files/d7/priv/sma14-4884.pdf

Sareen, J. (2014). Posttraumatic stress disorder in adults: impact, comorbidity, risk factors, and treatment. *Canadian Journal of Psychiatry, 59*(9), 460–467. https://doi.org/10.1177/070674371405900902

Sato, W., Kochiyama, T., Uono, S., Matsuda, K., Usui, K., Inoue, Y., & Toichi, M. (2011). Rapid amygdala gamma oscillations in response to fearful facial expressions. *Neuropsychologia, 49*(4), 612–617. https://doi .org/10.1016/j.neuropsychologia.2010.12.025

Seligman, M. E. P. (1975). *Helplessness: On depression, development, and death.* W. H. Freeman/Times Books/Henry Holt & Co.

Seymour, B., Daw, N., Dayan, P., Singer, T., & Dolan, R. (2007). Differential encoding of losses and gains in the human striatum. *Journal of Neuroscience, 27*(18), 4826–4831. https://doi.org/10.1523 /JNEUROSCI.0400-07.2007

Shapiro, F. (2014). The role of eye movement desensitization and reprocessing (EMDR) therapy in medicine: Addressing the psychological and physical symptoms stemming from adverse life experiences. *The Permanente Journal, 18*(1), 71–77. https://doi.org/10.7812/TPP/13-098

Shin, L. M., Rauch, S. L., & Pitman, R. K. (2006). Amygdala, medial prefrontal cortex, and hippocampal function in PTSD. *Annals of the New York Academy of Sciences, 1071*(1), 67–79. https://doi.org/10.1196/annals.1364.007

Sierra, M., & Berrios, G. E. (1998). Depersonalization: Neurobiological perspectives. *Biological Psychiatry, 44*(9), 898–908. https://doi.org/10.1016/s0006-3223(98)00015-8

Smith, K. E., & Pollak, S. D. (2020). Early life stress and development: Potential mechanisms for adverse outcomes. *Journal of Neurodevelopmental Disorders, 12*(34). https://doi.org/10.1186/s11689-020-09337-y

Spencer-Segal, J. L., & Akil, H. (2019). Glucocorticoids and resilience. *Hormones and Behavior, 111*, 131–134. https://doi.org/10.1016/j.yhbeh.2018.11.005

Steinberg, E. E., Gore, F., Heifets, B. D., Taylor, M. D., Norville, Z. C., Beier, K. T., Földy, C., Lerner, T. N., Luo, L., Deisseroth, K., & Malenka, R. C. (2020). Amygdala-midbrain connections modulate appetitive and aversive learning. *Neuron, 106*(6), 1026–1043.e9. https://doi.org/10.1016/j.neuron.2020.03.016

Suglia, S. F., Koenen, K. C., Boynton-Jarrett, R., Chan, P. S., Clark, C. J., Danese, A., Faith, M. S., Goldstein, B. I., Hayman, L. L., Isasi, C. R., Pratt, C. A., Slopen, N., Sumner, J. A., Turer, A., Turer, C. B., Zachariah, J. P., American Heart Association Council on Epidemiology and Prevention, Council on Cardiovascular Disease in the Young, Council on Functional Genomics and Translational Biology, Council on Cardiovascular and Stroke Nursing, & Council on Quality of Care and Outcomes Research (2018). Childhood and adolescent adversity and cardiometabolic outcomes: A scientific statement from the American Heart Association. *Circulation, 137*(5), e15–e28. https://doi.org/10.1161/CIR.0000000000000536

Swick, D., Cayton, J., Ashley, V., & Turken, A. U. (2017). Dissociation between working memory performance and proactive interference control in post-traumatic stress disorder. *Neuropsychologia, 96*, 111–121. https://doi.org/10.1016/j.neuropsychologia.2017.01.005

Terpou, B. A., Densmore, M., Théberge, J., Thome, J., Frewen, P., McKinnon, M. C., & Lanius, R. A. (2019). The threatful self: Midbrain functional connectivity to cortical midline and parietal regions during subliminal trauma-related processing in PTSD. *Chronic Stress, 3*. https://doi.org/10.1177/2470547019871369

Thandi, G., Tom, D., Gould, M., McKenna, P., & Greenberg, N. (2015). Impact of a single-session of havening. *Health Science Journal, 9*(5).

Tomasello, M. (2016). *A natural history of human morality.* Harvard University Press.

Truitt, K. (2022). *Healing in your hands: Self-havening practices to harness neuroplasticity, heal traumatic stress, and build resilience.* PESI Publishing.

Tsao, A., Moser, M. B., & Moser, E. I. (2013). Traces of experience in the lateral entorhinal cortex. *Current Biology, 23*(5), 399–405. https://doi.org/10.1016/j.cub.2013.01.036

Tuttle, R. H. (2022, November 30). Human evolution. In *Encyclopedia Britannica.* https://www.britannica.com/science/human-evolution

U.S. Department of Education. (2019). Student reports of bullying: Results from the 2017 School Crime Supplement to the National Crime Victimization Survey. *National Center for Education Statistic Reports.* https://nces.ed.gov/pubs2019/2019054.pdf

van der Kolk, B. A. (2014). *The body keeps the score: brain, mind, and body in the healing of trauma.* Viking.

Verwoerd, J., Wessel, I., & de Jong, P. J. (2009). Individual differences in experiencing intrusive memories: The role of the ability to resist proactive interference. *Journal of Behavior Therapy and Experimental Psychiatry, 40*(2), 189–201. https://doi.org/10.1016/j.jbtep.2008.08.002

von Bartheld, C. S., Bahney, J., & Herculano-Houzel, S. (2016). The search for true numbers of neurons and glial cells in the human brain: A review of 150 years of cell counting. *The Journal of Comparative Neurology, 524*(18), 3865–3895. https://doi.org/10.1002/cne.24040

Vyas, A., Jadhav, S., & Chattarji, S. (2006). Prolonged behavioral stress enhances synaptic connectivity in the basolateral amygdala. *Neuroscience, 143*(2), 387–393. https://doi.org/10.1016/j.neuroscience.2006.08.003

Vyas, A., Mitra, R., Shankaranarayana Rao, B. S., & Chattarji, S. (2002). Chronic stress induces contrasting patterns of dendritic remodeling in hippocampal and amygdaloid neurons. *The Journal of Neuroscience, 22*(15), 6810–6818. https://doi .org/10.1523/JNEUROSCI.22-15 -06810.2002

Wang, F., Pan, F., Shapiro, L. A., & Huang, J. H. (2017). Stress induced neuroplasticity and mental disorders. *Neural Plasticity,* 9634501. https:// doi.org/10.1155/2017/9634501

Wenzel, J. M., Oleson, E. B., Gove, W. N., Cole, A. B., Gyawali, U., Dantrassy, H. M., Bluett, R. J., Dryanovski, D. I., Stuber, G. D., Deisseroth, K., Mathur, B. N., Patel, S., Lupica, C. R., & Cheer, J. F. (2018). Phasic dopamine signals in the nucleus accumbens that cause active avoidance require endocannabinoid mobilization in the midbrain. *Current Biology, 28*(9), 1392–1404.e5. https://doi.org/10.1016/j.cub .2018.03.037

Wolfelt, A. (2016). *Counseling skills for companioning the mourner: The fundamentals of effective grief counseling.* Companion Press.

Zale, E. L., & Ditre, J. W. (2015). Pain-related fear, disability, and the fear-avoidance model of chronic pain. *Current Opinion in Psychology, 5,* 24–30. https://doi.org/10.1016/j.copsyc.2015.03.014

Zhang, Y., Xie, B., Chen, H., Li, M., Guo, X., & Chen, H. (2016). Disrupted resting-state insular subregions functional connectivity in post-traumatic stress disorder. *Medicine, 95*(27), e4083. https://doi .org/10.1097/MD.0000000000004083

Acknowledgments

This book has been a passion project of mine for many years. As a lump of clay waiting to be molded into its final form, it passed through many hands. My deepest gratitude goes out to all who sat with my story and provided critical feedback and support as it unfolded on these pages.

Thank you to the incredible scientists, researchers, and clinicians who brought to light the science I draw upon in this book. You are my inspiration and have brought me sanity when I struggled in the depths of my brain's own darkness.

My Naz. Thank you for your never-ending support, your generosity in sponsoring me to share our story, and for always honoring my past. You are my heart.

For my parents, thank you for all the things. I am so grateful that when I started writing this book you gave me your full support. I'll never forget shakily dropping off manuscripts for you and keeping my fingers crossed for a green light to share parts of our family's journey. Thank you for not only empowering me to break through the "fine" narrative of our family story but also encouraging me to boldly share the hard parts in service to humanity. I love you.

Sara, my chosen sister, thank you for being by my side through life's journey, in darkness and light. Decades of wit, wisdom, and love shared—thank you for *you*.

Drs. Ron and Steve Ruden, thank for your presence, friendship, and support. I adore our calls and deep dives into the nuances of the neurobiology of healing and thriving. Thank you for inviting me into your realm as a codeveloper of Havening and empowering me to walk alongside you as we bring Havening to humanity.

To my incredible teams: your dedication to empowering healing keeps me grounded and drives me to grow stronger and wiser daily. Your unwavering commitment to empowerment and healing is truly inspiring. This journey is a collective effort, and I'm grateful for every step we take together. A special acknowledgment to the heart and foundation of our group, Lorelei. My deepest thanks to you, Lorelei.

Rebecca, your care, support, and wisdom over the years—and especially in the creation of this manuscript—are invaluable gifts to me. Thank you for holding space, offering guidance, and sharing countless laughs and, at times, tears as I navigated and refined some of the most challenging parts of my story. You've helped me bring closure to so many loose ends.

Thank you to PESI for believing in me and this project. Kate Sample, you are an exceptional agent, and I am honored to be partnered with you on this extraordinary journey. Chelsea Thompson, you are an incredible editor. Thank you for the laughter we shared, the human moments and feedback that made this book better, and your wonderful care with my story.

About the Author

Dr. Kate Truitt is a licensed clinical psychologist and applied neuroscientist, and holds an MBA in healthcare administration. She is an internationally recognized expert in the neuroscience of trauma, stress, and resilience as well as the complex interplay among the three. She is regularly featured in global media outlets ranging from *Oprah Today* and *Medium* to the BBC and *Today*. Dr. Kate is an international trainer and has spoken at the United Nations, the United States Department of Defense, PESI, and others. She has dedicated her life to advancing the treatment of trauma and stress-related disorders, eliminating the stigma surrounding mental health, and empowering wellness through the dissemination of psychoeducation and self-healing tools within her speaking engagements, books, blog, and social media presence.

Dr. Kate resides in Los Angeles, CA, where she leads her flagship group practice and clinic, Dr. Kate Truitt & Associates. She serves as CEO for both the Amy Research Foundation, a non-profit focused on advancing the role of brain science in psychotherapy and eradicating the translational lag between science and clinical practice, and the Trauma Counseling Center of Los Angeles. In 2013, she founded the Truitt Institute (formerly known as Viva Excellence) to provide cutting-edge trainings and seminars that bring together the newest advancements in the fields of neuroscience and mental health. Dr. Kate is also a developer of the Havening Techniques and serves as their Chief Science Advisor.

Dr. Kate's NeuroTriad Model consists of three core pillars: trauma-informed, neuroscience-based, and resilience-focused care. Taken together, these components empower individuals to become proactive participants in their transformational journey as they heal the past, create the present, and build the future. She is the author of *Healing in Your Hands: Self-Havening Practices to Harness Neuroplasticity, Heal Traumatic Stress, and Build Resilience.*

You can find Dr. Kate on:

YouTube: https://www.youtube.com/c/DrKateTruitt

TikTok: https://www.tiktok.com/@dr.katetruitt

LinkedIn: https://www.linkedin.com/in/drkatetruitt

Instagram: https://www.instagram.com/dr.katetruitt

Facebook: https://www.facebook.com/DrKateTruitt